A BBC Radio 4 Book of the Week

'A wide-ranging, gloriously obsessive odyssey . . . a wonderful insight into the history, culture and sheer hard work taken to make this most fundamental of human foods. This book reminds us of bread's special significance and importance' Jenny Linford, author of *The Missing Ingredient*

'Rob Penn's enthusiasm for what he calls "the most symbolically evocative foodstuff" is so infectious and persuasive . . . a pleasingly evocative tale, told with the same rich descriptions and wistful asides that Penn bakes into all of his books' *Geographical*

'A Sapiens-with-wheat story of humanity: Far from being yet another book on how to achieve the perfect sourdough starter, Robert Penn's engaging account encompasses every aspect of bread, from how it fuelled entire empires to which grains he could grow on his own allotment' *Evening Standard*

'Compelling…a journey of discovery…The lesson he wanted to show his children, getting them to think about the concepts of self-reliance and limiting their exposure to the forces of the global economy by bringing the provenance of things closer to home, has been learnt' *Daily Telegraph*

'Never less than entertaining… a reminder of how remarkable bread is: familiar though it may be, a loaf of bread is also "an everyday miracle"' *Daily Mail*

'Compelling, vivid . . .[Penn] explores his enthusiasm for sourdough bread, and forgotten "landrace" wheats, as he supervises their planting, harvesting and the milling of the grain that would go into his loaf . . . *Slow Rise* will be welcomed by the new bread geeks' *Spectator*

'People keep rediscovering the joy of bread. In truth it never went away; it was just subverted by pappy cheaper bread . . . Robert Penn celebrates what we can do to reverse this culinary serfdom' Tim Lang, author of *Feeding Britain*

ABOUT THE AUTHOR

Robert Penn is a broadcaster, conservationist, lifelong cyclist and the author of several books including the *Sunday Times* bestseller *It's All About the Bike* and *The Man Who Made Things Out of Trees*. His books have been published in fourteen languages. He lives in the Black Mountains, South Wales with his wife, three children, two spaniels, twelve bicycles and a collection of sickles. He bakes his own bread in a wood-fired oven.

Slow Rise

A Bread-Making Adventure

ROBERT PENN

PENGUIN BOOKS

PENGUIN BOOKS

UK | USA | Canada | Ireland | Australia
India | New Zealand | South Africa

Penguin Books is part of the Penguin Random House group of companies
whose addresses can be found at global.penguinrandomhouse.com.

First published by Particular Books 2021
Published in Penguin Books 2022

001

Printed and bound in Great Britain by Clays Ltd, Elcograf S.p.A.

The authorized representative in the EEA is Penguin Random House Ireland,
Morrison Chambers, 32 Nassau Street, Dublin DO2 YH68

A CIP catalogue record for this book is available from the British Library

ISBN: 978-0-141-98855-9

www.greenpenguin.co.uk

Penguin Random House is committed to a
sustainable future for our business, our readers
and our planet. This book is made from Forest
Stewardship Council® certified paper.

For my mum,
who taught me long ago that sitting round
a table, breaking bread with the people you love, is
the best of life.

'With bread all sorrows are less'
– Miguel de Cervantes

Contents

Flour, Yeast, Water & Salt

'The need of the immaterial is the most deeply
rooted of all needs. One must have bread; but before
bread, one must have the ideal.' – Victor Hugo

Though Tarık Yıldız had the cherubic face of a small boy
staring out of an aeroplane window on a runway approach,
he drove the car like a getaway driver. We thundered down
the road to Siverek. The peaks of the Taurus Mountains
gleamed white against the azure Anatolian sky. Storm clouds
were gathering to the south over the Harran Plain, a great
sweep of rich, agricultural land with biblical resonance. We
passed small forestry plantations, pistachio and almond
orchards, variegated basins with irrigated fields and great,
bare plateaus where the wind reigned. As we sped north-east,
limestone hummocks gave way to hillsides of reddish, grey
and black basalt rocks. In places, the rocks had been piled up
into boundary walls, creating small fields the colour of dark
chocolate. Cresting one of the rolling ridges at speed, Tarık's
hands sprang off the wheel and pointed to the horizon. There
it was – a huge, horizontal arc of fractured volcanic rock pro-
truding from the skyline, like the vertebral column of a buried
stegosaurus – the Karacadağ massif.

Tarık is a friend of a friend of a friend. He grew up in the village of Örencik, near the city of Şanlıurfa, a stone's throw from Göbekli Tepe, one of the oldest and most extraordinary archaeological sites on the planet. Like the majority of the population in this corner of Anatolia, Tarık is an ethnic Kurd, the stateless nation of thirty million people who live across the high mountains and plains of Syria, Turkey, Iran and Iraq. I had recruited him to help me search for wild wheat on the slopes of Karacadağ And though he clearly thought the enterprise was strange, our distant alliance bound him to assist me. He also had an old friend from university who lived in the city of Siverek, near the foot of the massif we were to climb. Berzan Karadağ had a degree in archaeology. He would know the way not only to the summit, but also to the best restaurant in Siverek, for the celebratory dinner I had promised when we descended. Siverek, Tarık kept telling me, was famous for its bread.

Karacadağ rises over the apex of the Fertile Crescent, the sickle-shaped territory of the ancient world known as the 'cradle of civilization' that includes modern Iraq, western Iran, south-east Turkey, Syria, Lebanon, Israel, Jordan and Egypt. Some 15,000 years ago, part of this region was occupied by 'Natufians', a diverse community of hunter-gatherers united by a shared culture. Natufians were the first humans to adopt a semi-sedentary way of life, and the first people on earth to bake bread.

In 2017, the discovery of charred food remains in a fireplace at a hunter-gatherer site called Shubayqa 1, in a desolate area of eastern Jordan called the Black Desert, dated the preparation and consumption of flatbread-like products made from cereals and plant roots to around 14,400 years ago. Under analysis using scanning electron microscopes, the structure of the bread-like fragments in the remains indicated they had been extensively processed. Cereal and non-cereal components had been threshed, winnowed, milled and possibly sieved, before being mixed with water into a form of dough and cooked. Of course, the absence of evidence is not evidence of absence. Bread might have become part of the human diet even earlier, but as far as empirical data goes, this is the beginning of bread.

During the silent millennia, in the aeon of prehistory, humankind subsisted by hunting and gathering. We emerged as anatomically modern humans around 150,000 years ago and it is reasonable to assume we have been eating seeds from wild grasses ever since. Grasses from the Poaceae (or Gramineae) family, which occupy over half of the planet's habitable landmass, are particularly good at collecting solar energy and re-configuring it into a form of biomass that happens to be nourishing to us. Sorghum residues found on stone tools in a cave in Mozambique have been dated to 105,000 years ago. We know barley was in the diet of Neanderthals, the extinct subspecies of humans, 50,000 years ago. There is evidence that grinding stones, used for a variety of everyday chores including processing cereal grains, became common 15,000 years ago. Carbonized grain fragments found at sites throughout the Eastern Mediterranean show that wild wheats became part of the diet of hunter-gatherers around the same time, in the form of a rudimentary gruel or porridge of pounded grains mixed with water. It would have been a small step, and the logical finale to a sequence of cereal-related human activities – gathering seeds, grinding or crushing, then soaking and mixing – to actually baking bread, either on hot, flat stones, or in the ashes of a fire.

Shubayqa 1 was occupied by Natufians. In processing and baking wild cereal grains, they created a foodstuff that was more appealing in several ways. Bread would have smelt, looked and tasted better than the porridge they were familiar with. It would also have been easier to digest and more nutritious. Evidence from Shubayqa 1 and other archaeological sites in the region suggests bread was a rarity though, rather than a dietary staple. It might have been an elite foodstuff for the Natufians, prepared only on special occasions or for ceremonial purposes. Perhaps, because the process took time and energy, people couldn't be bothered to make bread regularly, rather like today.

The wheat plants collected around Shubayqa 1 and processed to make bread were wild grasses, part of a family of plants that grew in thick stands on heavy soils in the hill country of the Fertile Crescent. Slowly, over millennia, the Natufians came to rely on these wild grasses more and more, perhaps as the nomadic impulse of their ancestors began to fade. They manufactured better tools for harvesting them, including sickles with flint blades set in bone handles, and they followed the grasses to new areas, establishing their semi-permanent 'base camps' wherever plant food resources, particularly wild wheats and barley, were plentiful.

Around 10,000 BC, as the climate became warmer, wetter and more stable throughout the Fertile Crescent, two species of self-pollinating annual grasses, known to us today as wild einkorn and wild emmer, expanded their habitat and began to grow more profusely. Both these species of wheat produce 'heads' or 'ears' containing seeds attached to brittle stalks or 'rachides', which spontaneously shatter when ripe, spreading the seeds on the wind in order to germinate in the soil – a dispersal mechanism devised over hundreds of thousands of years, to ensure natural propagation. A single gene mutation in both species, however, produced a tough or non-shattering rachis that left the plump seeds attached to the ears of selected plants. Around 9,000 BC, proto-farmers began to gather these mutant ears of wheat, and plant them closer to their camps.

Over a long period of time, einkorn and emmer became domesticated crops, growing in a modified way that met with our nascent desire for more convenient and abundant food-stuffs. Thus, humans effectively reversed the means of natural propagation in these plants, in order to beget upon the earth more easily, and put bread on the table. The process of selection and propagation – in einkorn first, it is thought, then emmer – was the first human improvement in any plant, ever. We had taken reproductive control away from nature. The new varieties of domesticated wheat could only be propagated by man: the life of each, man and plant, had inadvertently become dependent upon the other. It signalled the advent of farming, and the beginning of what is known today as the 'Neolithic Revolution'.

By 7,000 BC, most of the wheat grown and harvested in the Near East was the non-shattering variety. The descend-ants of the Natufians, now living in permanent settlements,

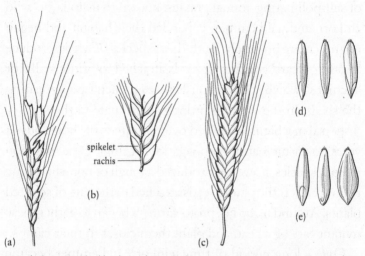

(a) & (b) A ripe ear of wild einkorn wheat: spikelets containing seeds separate easily from the brittle rachis when ripe. (c) A ripe ear of domesticated wheat: spikelets containing seeds remain on the ear until released by threshing. (d) Wild einkorn seeds. (e) Domesticated einkorn seeds.

started to hoe and plough, planting the grains deeper in the soil. They started to weed, irrigate and fertilize their fields. The cycle of growth, fruition, death and re-birth in plants, and the connection between this and the cycle of the seasons, the movement of the heavenly bodies and the rhythms of the weather, became profoundly interesting to them. In the succeeding millennia, the human population on earth has doubled ten times, from approximately five million to approaching eight billion, and ten billion soon. Most of the calories that permitted this increase have come from three plants: rice, maize and wheat. The oldest and most important of these is wheat. Wheat is the pre-eminent staple of humankind.

Wheat was not the only wild plant to provide the edible foundations of civilization in the Fertile Crescent, 10,000 years ago. According to long-standing archaeological consensus, the 'founder crops' were emmer, einkorn, barley, chickpea, bitter vetch, pea, lentil and flax, though it is now thought there may have been more. Einkorn and emmer, along with barley, were the earliest domesticates, though, and they offered several advantages from the start. They grew quickly, yielded well and were harvestable within a few months of sowing – an asset for bands of hunter-gatherers who were transitioning from nomadism to being settled villagers. The harvested crops could be readily processed into foodstuffs like gruel and bread, using technologies developed over previous millennia. Crucially, they could be stored for lengthy periods, enabling communities to survive times of dearth in other foodstuffs. They could also be transported and traded as raw materials. Finally, both einkorn and emmer, like the entire grass family, are self-pollinating.

The speed and means of the domestication process, across the Fertile Crescent at first, then outwards towards Asia, North Africa and Europe, are contentious. As the population in established farming communities grew, waves of farmer-colonizers left the Near East, taking with them their practices – sowing, husbandry, reaping and threshing – as well as their cereal culture of fermenting, baking and storing grain. At the same time, further plants fell within the scope of human cultivation. Digging sticks and primitive hoes evolved into ploughs, and dependence on nature's soils evolved through stages of careful preparation to planned enrichment. Around 7,000 BC, we had domesticated cattle – to which we fed grasses including however, is 'free-threshing' or 'naked' – the husk separates easily from the seed, a huge boon for the farmer. Bread wheat had other qualities too: the grains were larger and the rachides were stronger (and even less likely to blow away on the wind), while the genetic complexity of bread wheat meant it could tolerate more diverse climates. It also made great bread.

Despite all these advantages, bread wheat caught on surprisingly slowly. It took a few millennia before the Greeks and then the Romans finally adopted bread wheat, in preference to einkorn and emmer. From there, it steadily encircled the globe. Today, bread wheat accounts for 95 per cent of all the wheat grown on earth, covering an area of some two million square kilometres – more than any other food crop – providing food for 2.5 billion people. Bread wheat remains one of the most successful plants in history, even though it does not grow in the wild.

Exactly where the domestication of wild einkorn and wild emmer first took place was a mystery for a long time. Archaeology, archaeobotanical data, art depictions and ethnography all provide clues, which suggest the process occurred in different places within the Fertile Crescent simultaneously. Then, in the 1990s, advances in technology allowed geneticists to look at the equivalent sections of DNA within the chromosomes of different plants and compare their sequences. Having studied wild and domesticated varieties of einkorn and emmer from locations spanning central Europe to western Iran, the geneticists concluded that both the species of domesticated wheat had evolved in exactly the same place. Remarkably, the cultivated varieties of both emmer and einkorn are most closely related to populations of their wild ancestors that still grow together today, on the lower slopes of the same basalt volcano between the Euphrates and the Tigris rivers – the Karacadağ massif.

We collected Berzan from an agricultural showroom in Siverek. He was stout, red-bearded and Tolkienesque, with eyes that glittered like fish scales in crystal-clear water. As we raced on towards the volcano, he explained that he sold machinery because there was no money in archaeology. In the network of villages on the lower slopes of Karacadağ, basalt rocks cleared from fields had been built into cottages, cattle sheds, winter feed stores and animal pens. We stopped often. Berzan asked for directions and I flashed up images of wild einkorn and wild emmer plants on my phone. The summit of the mountain was this way or that way, the villagers said, and yes, these wheats do grow here, but not at this time of year. I had suspected the third week in October was too late. In south-east Anatolia, wheat ripens in June and dies back by early autumn. We searched the roadsides anyway. I walked among the desiccated wild grasses, looking for wheat seeds that might have been dispersed in their husks. Tarık and Berzan leant on the car bonnet, smoking white-tipped cigarettes.

Eventually, we found the village of Karacadağ – it means 'Deer Mountain' – and the road began to rise steeply, between rows of snow poles. The last of the grasses gave out to a rugged, sub-alpine scrub of hoary tussocks and thistles. We had to pull over to let a Turkish armoured military vehicle past, which unnerved me more than the two young Kurdish lads. Each bend in the road revealed another sweeping view of wild, treeless moorland. At the abandoned ski station – a single, broken drag lift and a café with boarded-up windows – we parked the car. To the consternation of Tarık, who was shod in black loafers, we set off to walk to the summit.

From the top at 1,957m, a series of rocky peaks – one with a meteorology station, another with a military observation post – rolled away to the south. The jagged, white-capped Kurdish Taurus Mountains arced round us along the northern horizon like a set of broken teeth. The city of Diyarbakır, cream-coloured in the weakening sun, looked like a misplaced jigsaw piece on the immutable plain where the Tigris River runs. When a cloud passed in front of the sun, the whole landscape, painted lightly by millennia of human endeavour, became distant, both physically and in time. Even the wind felt old.

Berzan pointed out the shepherd's camp below us, bedded into a moorland dimple beside a black tarn. These semi-nomadic people spend half the year on the upland pastures grazing their sheep and goats, he explained. In late autumn, they descend to their villages on the plains. This transhumance existence dates back to the beginning of civilization. Sheep and goats were first domesticated in the Fertile Crescent around the same time as wheat. We watched the kids scampering between the tents like ants. Their faint cries just reached us on the lip of the wind. Did women from the camp, I wondered, still gather the seeds of the ancestral wild einkorn and emmer plants at the bottom of the mountain, and make bread to feed their families? Berzan did not know, but it struck me as likely. In the late 1960s, Jack Harlan, the American botanist and plant breeding's answer to Indiana Jones, walked across the lower slopes of Karacadağ, through massive stands of wild wheat, stripping seed heads by hand at first, and then with a flint sickle. In an hour, he harvested two kilos of wild emmer. Later, he calculated that a family could readily gather enough wild cereals to last them for a year, in just three weeks.

Why humans switched from hunting and gathering to farming is one of the most important questions in our history, and we don't know the answer. There are many theories. Harlan believed that the shift from an exclusively hunter-gatherer lifestyle to one that entailed harvesting cereals took place because the abundance was such an attractive alternative to the uncertainty of hunting. V. G. Childe, the great Australian archaeologist who coined the term 'Neolithic Revolution' in 1923, adhered to the idea that climate change first drove our species to agriculture. Some demographers believe that population growth within communities of hunter-gatherers created pressure to grow more food per unit of land. Anthropologists have argued that we first became sedentary in order to feast and partake in rituals at communal complexes like Göbekli Tepe, 100 kilometres away and within sight of Karacadağ on a clear day; the domestication of crops inevitably followed. Maybe the big game ran out. Maybe we lost the nomadic impulse. It's possible we simply fell in love with bread and wanted more.

A fire was burning in the shepherd's camp below us now. The ascent of man is a deceptive show, I thought; their nomadic way of life has changed little over ten millennia. Perhaps – it was a wild notion, but I was faint from surveying the prehistoric landscape – perhaps it was an ancestor of these shepherds who walked through a sward of wild grasses on the slopes below us and, one June morning 11,000 years ago, first stripped an intact ear of mutant wheat, to take home to make bread. Perhaps he or, more likely, she then rubbed the ear between her hands and, in a moment of contemplation, saw in that palm of golden seeds a glimmer of humankind's teeming cities, the spires of cathedrals, the libraries of knowledge, rockets soaring to the moon and even intelligent machines. Perhaps she clasped her fingers round the seeds, took them back to camp and planted them – a simple domestic act that initiated tumultuous changes to human society and the environment, the consequences of which now imperil us. It was a pivotal moment in life on earth. With that act, the Pleistocene, the prodigious epoch of prehistory that began 2.6 million years ago, ended. The Anthropocene began. I articulated this thought to Tarık. His thick, black eyebrows rose and parted. He scuffed a rock with his loafer and said: 'Robert, Berzan is hungry.'

The light was fading faster than Tarık's patience. It was obvious we were not going to find wild einkorn and wild emmer on the slopes of Karacadağ today. Dinner, and a platter of Siverek's famous breads, had renewed appeal.

I was raised on industrial bread. My mum is an excellent cook – she even ran her own catering business for a while – but she worked full-time when I was young and the convenience of 'medium sliced white' was too great to resist. My brother and I ate loaves of Mother's Pride and Sunblest by the baker's dozen. Occasionally, we ate an entire loaf in a sitting. For years, our first port of call in the kitchen was the beige bread bin; on tiptoes, on a stool, I would hook an arm over and blindly feel for the spongy, cellophane-wrapped rectangular lump, like the claw machine in a fairground arcade. I was briefly captivated by Ridley Scott's famous 1973 TV commercial for Hovis – a bread delivery boy pushing a bicycle up a cobbled lane to Dvořák's 'New World' Symphony – but I never ate the brown bread it advertised. It was nutrient-stripped white – white enough to blind you – or nothing at all: white toast and honey for breakfast; white bread to mop up liver and bacon stew at lunchtime; white toast with Marmite and baked beans in front of *Grange Hill* for tea. When Mum cooked one of her signature Indian curries, she handmade rotis, parathas and naan breads, but she never thought to bake our daily bread. We didn't know anyone who ate home-made bread. At the end of a lane on the edge of a village in the English West Midlands, I had no idea that the idealists of 1960s counterculture in California viewed the type of bread we ate as the edible embodiment of everything that was wrong with modern America. There was no copy of James Beard's 1973 *Beard on Bread*, the bellwether for a new culinary conscience, in our local library. When the New York arbiter of style Diane Vreeland wrote in the early 70s, 'People who eat white bread have no dreams,' nobody came down our lane to tell us.

At university in the late 1980s, medium-sliced, white velvet slivers of tasteless bread remained a pillar of my diet. I ate it perfunctorily, like the state workers who built the pyramids in pharaonic Egypt or the peasants who tilled fields in medieval England. Still, no one pointed out that modern, industrial bread – a product of technology, of standardized-flour quality and fast-rising yeasts, of mechanical mixers and automatic ovens – was an ignoble imitation of the sacred foodstuff our ancestors survived on. Working in an office in London in the 1990s, bread continued to provide a significant component of my carbohydrate intake. The delis in Covent Garden, where I bought a sandwich every lunchtime, offered novel fillings like avocado, salsa and bacon or smoked salmon and cream cheese, which hinted at the emergence of a British cuisine beyond boiled bacon and Angel Delight. The bread, though, was still as white as new road markings, and pre-sliced. Then I went travelling. Cycling round the world for three years, I ate more good bread than I had done in the previous twenty-seven years. I consumed bagels and corn bread, pumpernickel and tortillas, date bread, onion bread, *lavash*, Hungarian potato bread, Georgian *puri*, chapattis and pitta. Pedalling through Iran, I devoured *sangak* and *nan-e barbari*. In Turkey, I carbo-loaded on *gözleme* and *simit*. Crossing Europe, I marvelled at all the regional breads I had never heard of – *grissini*, *fougasse*, Macedonian *pogacha*, *Bauernbrot* and rye sourdough, to name a few.

Back in London at the end of the millennium, it was at least possible to buy good bread, or 'real bread' as it began to be called. My local wholefood shop in Brixton sold hefty wholemeal loaves. A mile from my flat, the capital's oldest organic bakery, the Old Post Office, produced first-class rye and sour-dough breads. Then my wife and I moved to the Black Mountains in Wales. We had three kids in a hurry. Craft baking had not filtered out of the cities into rural Britain and we forgot about real bread. We surrendered, as Mum had done in the 1970s, to expediency. We all ate superabundant, low-cost, cellophane-wrapped loaves bought in supermarkets on weekly shops. Then I fell ill.

Cycling round the world, eating at the roadside and drinking untreated water, I had worked my way through a litany of intestinal complaints including bacillary dysentery, amoebic dysentery and giardiasis. I wondered if one of these illnesses had come back to haunt me in my forties. Amoebic dysentery, for example, can lie dormant in the human gut for years. I had tests. They were inconclusive. I read more about the stability of bacteria in the gut and foodstuffs that disrupt it. I started to look at my diet, which I had always thought to be balanced and nutritionally wholesome. One day, my wife wondered out loud if I had coeliac disease, a serious autoimmune disorder that affects around one per cent of the population, whereby the ingestion of a protein found in bread called gluten leads to damage in the small intestine. Symptoms of coeliac disease vary from person to person, and diagnosis rates are increasing all over the world. I read more about gluten, one of the most heavily consumed proteins on earth. It is formed in bread dough as two proteins naturally stored in wheat seeds bond, when mixed with water during fermentation. The test for coeliac disease was negative.

Then I read *Bread Matters*, by Andrew Whitley, the baker and godfather of the 'Real Bread Campaign'. He wrote:

> British bread is a nutritional, culinary, social and environmental mess – made from aggressively hybridized wheat that is grown in soils of diminishing natural fertility, sprayed with toxins to counter pests and diseases, milled in a way that robs it of the best part of its nutrients, fortified with just two minerals and two vitamins in a vain attempt to make good the damage, and made into bread using a cocktail of functional additives and a super-fast fermentation (based on greatly increased amounts of yeast), which inhibits assimilation of some of the remaining nutrients while causing digestive discomfort to many consumers.

And, though I had never been on a diet or even considered proscribing a single foodstuff, I gave up eating bread. I did not remove gluten from my diet entirely: that is difficult these days. Since the 1970s, gluten has become a hidden ingredient in thousands of food products including pasta, breakfast cereals, cakes, biscuits, soups, ready meals, nutritional drinks, sausages and cosmetics, not that I eat cosmetics. I simply stopped eating industrial bread, and the era of my stomach ailments ended.

Just as the novelty of feeling well was wearing off, a neighbour gifted our household a tub of natural 'sourdough starter', the alchemical leavening agent used in bread baking for millennia. My wife quickly learnt to bake excellent, slow-fermented sourdough bread, made with nothing more than flour, water, salt and natural starter. Our children devoured it. I had read, by this time, about the health benefits of slow fermentation: it slows down the body's absorption of starch and helps break down gluten proteins, making them more digestible. Some researchers believe the increase in gluten intolerance and coeliac disease in the last half-century is related to the fact that industrial bread is fermented in a trice. Still, I initially suppressed the urge to eat my wife's bread. I learnt to bake instead. Pulling my own sweet-smelling loaves from the oven to feed hungry kids, I felt like Odysseus bound to the mast of his galley as it sailed past the island of the Sirens, with their seductive song. It wasn't long before I decided to risk rowing myself on to the rocks. I began eating bread again – real bread. It felt good in the hand, and it tasted great. Miraculously, it did not upset my stomach.

I quickly became absorbed by the baking process. Loaf by loaf, my bread got better. The emotional and psychological benefits of baking bread soon surpassed the physical pleasure of eating it. I read about the symbiotic relationship between the baker and the millions of impalpable microorganisms harnessed during fermentation. I fell in love with the feel of dough, and the meditative nature of kneading it. As the great American food writer M. F. K. Fisher, an early denouncer of industrial bread, wrote: homemade bread 'will smell better and taste better than you remembered anything could possibly taste or smell, and it will make you feel, for a time at least, newborn into a better world than this one often seems'.

At first, I used standard white flour bought in a supermarket. The next step was organic 'strong' white bread flour. Then I stumbled across the UK's network of small flour mills that produce the ingredients fuelling the revival in craft baking. I became interested in different flavours and textures. I made loaves with brown flour, malted flour, bio-dynamic organic spelt flour and rye flour (which my children refused to eat).

As my understanding of the baking process deepened, I started to learn about the history of bread. This was revelatory. Bread is one of the staple foods of humankind – the 'Staff of Life', as it was first dubbed in the seventeenth century – but I had no idea that a single foodstuff could have such a colossal impact on our progress as a species. From the first steps in the ascent of man, bread has empowered us immeasurably. The history of human civilization has been crowded into a few thousand years: bread has been a constant over this period. Bread is kneaded into economics, politics, human biology and religion. The availability of bread has significantly influenced demography and population growth. Its story is the story of humanity.

From the advent of the Neolithic Revolution on the slopes of the Karacadağ massif, bread has formed the nutritional and economic base of civilizations. Long before money, bread was wealth, and control of bread meant political power. The prosperity of Uruk, believed to be the first city by some archae-ologists, was based on barley bread. In ancient Egypt, bread was the most important element in the national diet and state workers' wages were paid partly in loaves. In ancient Rome, the government distributed a monthly dole of subsidized or free grain and later bread, to poorer citizens, to keep order and win votes. In recognition of the nutritional and ideological importance of bread in medieval England, the Assize of Bread was passed in 1266; this statute, the first law on food, officially tied the weight of a loaf to the price of grain for the first time (thereby enshrining the close link between bread and money). It was designed to ensure that bread be sold at a reasonable price. Remarkably, it remained law until the early nineteenth century. Then, the price of grain and the availability of cheap bread to fuel the industrialization of Britain was at the heart of a feud between the landed aristocracy and the arriviste factory owners, about protectionism versus free trade, which caused a colossal perturbation in Parliament leading to the Repeal of the Corn Laws in 1846. Before that, across the Channel, bread, or the lack of, was a catalyst in the political chain reaction that led to the French Revolution in 1789: 'No talk! Bread!' the sans-culotte mob cried. In the twentieth century, Stalin's dogmatic desire to keep exporting wheat at all costs ensured that millions starved to death from a dearth of bread in the early 1930s. More recently, during the 2011 uprising in Egypt, part of the Arab Spring, images of bread, as a standard under which people could rally and a symbol of something worth fighting for, were everywhere at the demonstrations.

The need to maintain an adequate supply of bread forged patterns of technological progress, through the refinement of tools at first, then via the use of power (particularly the Vitruvian watermill), and finally in the development of large-scale production. Similarly, it prompted key advances in agriculture like the 'Norfolk four-course crop rotation', and progress in the scientific discipline of plant hybridization. The need for bread also drove the evolution of global trade and commodity markets. Bread, inevitably, has been a determining factor in wars. As the Russian proverb says: 'Bread is the army's greatest ally: the soldier marches no farther than his stomach.' Or as Napoleon Bonaparte, who militarized bread production with his field bakeries and a cohort of flour engineers or *sapeurs blancs*, put it in 1807: 'To defeat the Russians is child's play, provided I can get bread.' During the American Civil War, the North had wheat and the South had cotton: bread spelt victory for the Union Army.

For many, 'life' and 'bread' were synonymous terms. A range of myths from diverse cultures portray bread as a divine gift to humanity. 'Bread' and 'dough' are slang terms for money in many languages – the 'breadwinner', or *gagne-pain* in French, brings money home to support the family – while 'bread' means 'food' in general (as in 'putting bread on the table') in many more. Though the term 'breadline' was not coined until the end of the nineteenth century, bread has been the ultimate staple commodity, marking the parameters of survival for the mass of people, for most of history.

The nutritional value and ubiquity of bread have caused it to accumulate great symbolic power across cultures and religions, wherever it is eaten. Representing everything from hope and honest toil to wealth and well-being, bread may even be the most symbolically evocative foodstuff of all. At the Last Supper, Jesus Christ gave bread to his disciples and said: 'Take, eat: this is my body,' creating one of the most powerful symbols in the sacred writings of any religion, at any time in history. There are – or at least were, until the homogenization of cultures in the twentieth century – symbolic breads to celebrate all the major annual calendar events. Most cultures have also devised breads to symbolize key transitional moments in the human life cycle. Notable among them are 'wedding breads', which have historic roots in many countries. Bread is frequently designed to be shared and it is bound up with basic human values like sociability: breaking bread with others signifies friendship and trust. Bread remains a fundamental part of the traditional welcome households offer to visitors in many countries. Numerous types of loaves are representative of the societies that bake them, while the bread we eat (or don't eat) still says a lot about who we are. In fact, with the rising tide of gluten sensitivity in the developed world and the return to craft baking, bread is a surprisingly contemporary story.

To ferment my fascination, I started to read about wheat, the most important plant in the story of bread. I studied articles by John Letts, an archaeobotanist and cereal farmer who specializes in growing 'heritage' varieties of wheat that predate modern agriculture. John has spearheaded a quiet movement of farmers, millers, bakers and bread eaters in the UK who are growing and processing varieties of wheat that make flavoursome bread, rather than solely delivering high yields. I read about micronutrients in soil and terroir in flour. Then it occurred to me: how can you make good bread without knowing the wheat variety?

Discovering heritage wheats was like entering Doctor Who's Tardis, with its infinite corridors and rooms. I found a website called 'Brockwell Bake Wheat: Gateway', maintained by Andy Forbes, a grower and baker-activist. The website consolidates publicly available data on over 400,000 wheat 'accessions' or entries in gene banks from around the world, which humans have grown throughout the ages. Andy also grows some of these heritage wheats in allotments, school grounds and parks across south London.

You can grow wheat on an allotment? This was a thunderbolt. I thought you needed a prairie. On the website, there were photos of small stands of wheat emerging on roof gardens, and primary-school kids tending plants in raised beds the size of bath tubs. One Saturday afternoon that autumn, I found myself with Andy in Ruskin Park, Lambeth, watching a pair of draught-horses called Heath and Nobby plough a patch of grass the size of a tennis court, in preparation for the planting of heritage grains. Could I grow my own wheat, too? I wondered. It was an obvious next step, to gratify my developing obsession. I asked Andy, as we were sowing seeds. He swept his long hair back, sucked on a rolled cigarette and purred.

Bread is an everyday miracle by which photons of light, nutrients in the soil and a bit of human toil become something delicious to eat. It is a reminder of the earth's abundance. Growing my own wheat might prompt me to give more thought to this; and, as bread is a lens on our relationship with many foodstuffs, possibly more thought to food in general. I had a quote from *The Grapes of Wrath* by John Steinbeck pinned on a board above my desk:

> And when that crop grew, and was harvested, no man had crumbled a hot clod in his fingers and let the earth sift past his fingertips. No man had touched the seed, or lusted for the growth. Men ate what they had not raised, had no

connection with the bread. The land bore under iron, and under iron gradually died; for it was not loved or hated; it had no prayers or curses.

The twentieth century was the first century since civilization began when the majority of us were not steeped in growing and harvesting cereals, then threshing, milling, baking and eating bread. Time was when the harvest was the future, and, for many, the story too. Perhaps growing wheat traditionally would release some biological valve deep within me, which the modern era has served to obstruct.

I live in deep countryside, in an old farmhouse surrounded by fields and woods. I don't own any farmland, but I know enough farmers: surely, I could rent an acre for a year. I could plant and harvest wheat by hand, then thresh it in my barn. I could mill the grain in one of the small working watermills in Wales. Finally, I could build a bread oven and bake bread at home for my family. As I would rather eat solar energy than oil, I would eschew the use of fertilizers, herbicides and pesticides. If industrial bread is part of a food system that offers convenience, superabundance, low cost and consumer choice, I wanted the opposite. I would make bread that is inconvenient, in limited supply, expensive (at least when you cost in my time) and without choice. Perhaps I could grow enough wheat to feed bread to my family for a year? Current national estimates for Wales state that the average person eats 580g of bread a week, or 30kg a year – a fraction of what we ate in the past. Miscellaneous sources from a century ago evidence that British people then ate closer to 150kg of bread a year, while anecdotal evidence from the eighteenth century suggests consumption was double that again. I did my own calculations, based on how much flour my wife and I use a week: I would need around 80kg of flour to keep the family in sourdough bread for a year. Surely, I could grow that amount.

I put the idea to my wife. She is interested in the concepts of self-reliance; of wresting freedom from everyday necessity; of limiting our exposure, as a family, to the bewildering forces of the global economy by bringing the provenance of things closer to home. She is particularly intent on confronting these issues on a quotidian basis, in the kitchen. For her, the act of baking is also a small protest – a declaration of domestic independence, from the corporations that seek complete control of a food system that has created an extraordinary plethora of environmental problems, as well as intractable human health issues. As the German proverb states: 'Whose bread I eat, his song I sing.' We are not above criticism, but we buy the minute amount of meat we eat from a smallholder nearby. We grow some of our own vegetables and buy the rest from an organic farm, also nearby. We avoid processed foods as much as we can. Why not plant our own wheat? My wife, though, had reservations. She knows I am susceptible to nostalgia for a way of life that ended two centuries ago. Also, our property is littered with the quietly eroding detritus of my previous obsessions.

'Oh dear,' she said. 'I seem to be married to a middle-aged man with a Thoreau complex. Do you really want us all to live like Amish farmers?' I did not speak out, but my heart danced. The answer, unequivocally, was yes.

CHAPTER I

Grain of Truth: Sowing

'History celebrates the battlefields whereon we meet
our death, but scorns to speak of the plowed fields
whereby we thrive; it knows the names of the King's
bastards, but cannot tell us the origin of wheat. That
is the way of human folly.' – J. Henri Fabre

'Walk up. Steady, steady. Whoa!' Roger Smith said, grasping
the plough handles. Betsy, a Clydesdale-Cob cross, and Alf,
a partially blind Gypsy Cob, came to a halt. The horses
bumped noses, snorted and shook their manes. Roger cast an
eye over the line in the earth behind him. He was 'putting a
scratch up,' he said, or inscribing a marker straight down the
middle of my acre, for when we started ploughing.

Nick Powell, a yeoman farmer and friend, had lent me the
acre for a year. It was an oblong plot in the corner of a 22-acre
field bordering a railway line, three miles from my home. It
was almost a 'selion', the medieval term for a strip of land
used for growing crops and typically one 'furlong' (660 feet)
long and one 'chain' (66 feet) wide. The earth was chestnut
brown. Sprigs of grass and weeds intermingled with last year's
stubble. Stout and bald, with hands like salted leather, Nick
grows wheat for money. He had already planted the other 21
acres and his seed had germinated, providing an iridescent,

green frame to my barren plot. Five hundred metres down the rolling slope and out of sight was the River Usk, a swollen, brown funnel of water at this time of year, winding out of the Welsh hills. Beyond that was the Blorenge, a heather-clad, sentinel peak at the eastern end of the Brecon Beacons, sculpted by glaciers during the last Ice Age. Further away to the north was Sugar Loaf or 'Y Fâl' in Welsh, a conical, purple-headed mountain so perfect it could have sprung from the imagination of an Edwardian schoolchild.

Roger replaced the 'coping sheer', used to scratch the centreline, with a proper ploughshare, before inspecting the horses' collars and adjusting the wheel height on the plough. He rolled the sleeves of his collarless shirt into tight knots above the elbow.

'We're ready to throw the first furrow up. Walk on,' Roger said. As the horses stepped forward, the traces snapped taut and the ploughshare sliced into the earth. With arms outstretched and hands fastened to the wooden handles, Roger lurched down the field like a sailor staggering across the quarterdeck of a ship in a roaring storm. The earth, cut by the 'coulter' or knife, was folded out to the side by the mouldboard, leaving a trench of exposed soil between Roger's feet.

Roger was born on a farm in the Black Mountains sixty years ago. He took the bus to school with my neighbour – 'when I went to school, that is,' he said. His father, Vear Smith, used horses on the farm into the 1960s, for planting swedes and potatoes, 'cleaning out' weeds and sowing cereals. Horses suited the hilly terrain and 'money was tight'. Tractors did eventually prevail, but Vear kept his hand in, competing at,

The action of the plough

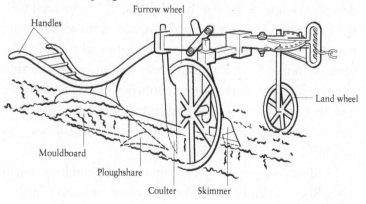

Handles

Furrow wheel

Land wheel

Mouldboard

Ploughshare

Coulter

Skimmer

and frequently winning, local horse-ploughing matches. Eventually, the plough, the tack, the horses and the weight of an ancestral tradition that had consecrated the land for centuries, passed down to Roger.

When we first spoke, at a ploughing match, Roger recalled customs like taking the plough into church for a blessing, and ploughing a 'corn dolly', made from the previous year's wheat, into the soil – a pagan prayer for a good harvest, and plentiful bread. His childhood farm had a threshing barn and a granary with a roller mill, used for milling oats for the animals and wheat flour for bread. Roger's mother baked bread twice a week in a brick oven, in a corner of the kitchen, which she lit with twig-firelighters called 'faggots'. She also made butter. It was, he said, the era 'before time became precious'.

I had gone to that ploughing match hoping to hire a team of horses and a ploughman. I had not expected to meet a character from the pages of a George Eliot novel. Roger described a way of life that had, I thought, disappeared with the Enclosure Acts, yet these experiences were within living memory. What I was proposing to do – grow wheat and make bread at home for my family – was not an enterprise that connected me to dark, distant centuries. It was how Roger and his family lived, in the 1960s, just before I was born. Not long before that, it was how everyone in the British country-side lived.

I had read that a good ploughman could plough an acre in a day. Roger qualified that: 'Yes, if he started at 5 a.m., finished at 10 p.m. and had three teams of horses.' Our plan was to plough half an acre. We made a good start. The horses were fresh. We were eager. The strip of neat furrows down the middle of the plot expanded quickly. Then the ploughshare broke, on a rock. As we were changing it, swollen clouds came over the mountains and burst on us. The rain began to fall in gunmetal-grey curtains. We put coats on. Then we put over-trousers, caps and more coats on. Shrouds of steam rose from Betsy and Alf. The furrows filled with water. The earth turned to a mud paste and our boots grew heavy. The joy of throwing that first one up faded.

When the rain eased, Roger suggested I have a turn. The key to ploughing is to hold a steady line, but it is difficult. Roger patiently offered advice. Even with the heavy horses taking the strain, it was hard work. I lugged, tugged, hoisted and heaved on the handles, to counter the forces the earth exerted on the mouldboard. After ten minutes, I discovered new muscles in my lower back. After an hour, I was exhausted.

I felt like I'd been in a wrestling bout. I had read that you walk eleven miles to plough an acre, and I knew I would not be able to stand up straight the following day. You can always spot a ploughman from his skewed gait, they used to say. I recalled Robert Burns, the Bard of Ayrshire, who was renowned for his 'ploughman's stoop', following years of manual labour in the fields. As Roger took over again, he said: 'You won't need anyone to rock you to sleep tonight.'

By 4 p.m., Alf was getting tired or bored, or both. When the rain began with purpose again, we called it. The horses knew immediately. Roger removed the bridles – it is bad luck not to put the bridle on last and take it off first, he explained – and the horses snorted. Almost half an acre had been transformed. A ragged carpet of stubble and weeds was now an oblong of orderly, parallel furrow-lines converging in the distance. Silver light bounced off the smooth, upturned ridges of plough-sheared earth. Roger was not content. Some of the furrows – mine, of course, though he was too polite to say so – oscillated wildly in the middle. In others, the furrow walls had collapsed. You would drop marks for this in a ploughing match.

Roger took apart the tack. I wondered why ploughmen put such emphasis on straightness and uniformity. As soon as I had sown my wheat, I was going to turn the furrows in anyway, to cover the seeds. There is virtue in a straight line, though. In a field, it is a measure of the ploughman's concentration, effort, honesty and skill. There is also an aesthetic quality in the sym-metry of ploughed earth. Looking down at the glistening rows again, I thought of John Stewart Collis, the writer and ecolo-gist. In *The Worm Forgives the Plough*, his memoir of working the land in the middle of the twentieth century, he described the straight furrow as 'the tribute that Agriculture pays to Art'.

When the tack was hung up and the horses had been fed, Roger led them into the back of the truck. The rain stopped. The wind picked up. The talons of the bare ash trees across the lane shook. Oak leaves curled around us. I thought about the winter ahead. My wife says I obsess about the weather needlessly. Now I had cause to. Rolling his sodden sleeves down, Roger looked over the field one last time and pursed his lips.

'Now, what are you going to plant, then?' he said.

Roger had never heard of emmer. Nor had I until I became interested in bread. Following domestication on the Karacadağ massif, emmer was the most abundant wheat variety in the Fertile Crescent for several thousand years. Some 8,500 years ago, it began to spread from the Fertile Crescent, presumably as seeds in the pockets of Neolithic frontiersmen and traders, across Iran to Asia, south through Mesopotamia and west across Anatolia to Europe. Around 6,000 years ago, emmer was first cultivated in Egypt. A millennium or so after that, it was being sown in southern Britain, where it remained the most important cereal until the beginning of the Bronze Age. By the time emmer reached India and then China 4,000 years ago, it was the dominant cereal on the planet.

In ancient Egypt, emmer had a special place in the diet. It was the main wheat cultivated for at least three millennia. Along with barley, it was a key ingredient of the pharaonic staples, bread and beer. In fact, it is thought that the first ever sourdough loaf was baked in Egypt, with emmer flour. Even though neighbouring countries grew other varieties of wheat during this period, emmer remained prevalent in Egypt, as Herodotus noted in the fifth century BC: 'while other nations live on naked wheat and barley, it is considered in Egypt the greatest shame to live on them'. We don't know if this was an agricultural, culinary or cultural preference. Nonetheless, the preference crossed the Mediterranean Sea and passed into classical times. The historian Cato the Elder wrote about the inclusion of emmer in sacrifices to the gods in the second century BC. In his encyclopaedic work *Naturalis Historia*, published in the first century AD, Pliny the Elder quotes an earlier Roman scholar who wrote: 'emmer was the only cereal used by the Roman nation for three hundred years'. For most of Roman history, marriage was made solemn when the bride and groom broke and ate a loaf of emmer. The Latin word for emmer, *far*, has reached us in *farina* and *farine*, respectively the modern Italian and French words for flour, and even in English terms like 'farinaceous'.

The cultivation of emmer declined with the Fall of Rome in the fifth century AD. Other varieties of 'free-threshing' wheat were easier to convert into flour. This wheat from antiquity lingered, though, in the marginal lands and mountainous areas across a wide geographic area spanning Europe and the Near East. As the centuries churned, emmer gained a reputation for resistance to certain fungal diseases, producing good yields on poor soils and tolerating climatic extremes. In 1901, M. A. Carleton, the American plant pathologist who did so much to improve wheat on the Great Plains of the USA, noted emmer's ability 'to make a good crop with almost any condition of soil or climate'. By the middle of the twentieth century, emmer had become a relic crop grown in remote outposts of Armenia, Albania, Spain, Italy, Iran, Morocco, the Carpathian Mountains of central Europe, the Volga region of Russia, and Ethiopia. Recently, emmer has made a small comeback, along with other ancient grains, as a speciality flour for baking tasty bread, and as a versatile, high-fibre health food, in shops and on vogueish restaurant menus. Many believe that these ancient grains are more easily digested than modern wheat varieties. Today, emmer is grown on a very small scale across the temperate world, from the USA to the Kars region, on the border between Turkey, Armenia and Iran.

When I first read about emmer, I began to see it everywhere. It was like learning a new word that then appears with improbable regularity, a cognitive phenomenon called 'frequency illusion'. I found packets of whole emmer grains on the shelves in my local health-food shop. I discovered recipes for emmer loaves in books on baking that I had thumbed through many times. I knew I was on a roll when I opened the menu at a restaurant in Lucca, a medieval walled city in central Italy, and *minestra di farro* – whole grained emmer soup – was a starter. *Farro* has been planted in parts of Tuscany continuously since Roman times, the waiter explained. Actually, emmer is *farro medio*, referring to the size of the grain. The other ancient hulled wheats, einkorn (*farro piccolo*) and spelt (*farro grande*), also fall within the broader term. Emmer, though, has ingrained its way most successfully into the Tuscan palate, featuring in peasant soups, salads, pasta dishes, biscuits and, of course, bread. In the mountainous Garfagnana area north of Lucca, emmer is grown by farmers as an IGP (Indicazione Geografica Protetta) product, with its geographic identity protected by law. Two days after my dinner in Lucca, cycling over the Apennine Mountains in Tuscany, I ate emmer bread for the first time. I stopped for a sandwich in a bar on the Passo della Raticosa, on the old road between Florence and Bologna. The owner gave me a choice: I could have a slab of pecorino cheese either in a white roll, or between thick-cut slices of *pane di farro* that she had baked that morning. With the first earthy, satisfying bite, I was sold.

The frequency illusion became dizzying when, a few weeks later, I was on a train across Britain reading a book on bread. The lady opposite, with eyes like an owl's and a great osprey's nest of white hair, introduced herself and told me that, during a visit to the Royal Botanic Gardens at Kew twenty years ago, she had seen emmer grain that was unearthed from the tombs of the pharaohs. Ancient Egyptian funeral rites, she explained, often included wheat offerings as food and possibly good-luck charms for the dead, on their journey through the afterlife. I scarcely believed her, but after one phone call, several emails and another train journey, I was sitting in an office at Kew with a variety of artefacts from the Economic Botany Collection on a table in front of me. There was a vial of orangey-brown emmer spikelets (a botanical term for the basic unit of a grass flower) from 'Rameside tomb, Egypt, *c.*1350 BC', emmer husks from 'Tel el Amarna' also dated to *c.*1350 BC, and a wooden frame containing ears of barley and durum wheat from the Greco-Roman period, in the first century BC. Most riveting of all was an 8cm by 5cm cardboard dish – Cat. No. 40592 – containing

Painstaking excavation has since revealed a site of great antiquity and importance. Göbekli Tepe comprises a complex of 'monumental' buildings erected by hunter-gatherers between 9600 and 8200 BC. The buildings, which pre-date the Great Pyramid at Giza by almost 6,000 years, display a remarkable level of architectural sophistication, skilled artisanship and collective enterprise.

I had spent the morning exploring the site. Though I had read about it, I was not prepared for the sense of ambition and communality, the intimate scale of the almost crypt-like buildings and the tenderness of the low-relief carvings that together provide an opaque window on our early spiritual development. I thought about the anxiety of the people who lived here, their yearning for order in a convulsing world and their search for meaning at a pivotal moment in history, as humans changed from being hunter-gatherers to domesticated farmers. Building Göbekli Tepe was clearly a massive undertaking, played out over centuries. The community of stonemasons, artists and labourers who worked there would have required a continuous supply of food to sustain them, which means cereals were probably cultivated in the very black soil the Yıldız family now farm, from the beginning of the Neolithic Revolution.

Mahmut politely offered me the wheel of the tractor, to have a go at ploughing. Instead, I sat on the wall of basalt rocks along the field boundary and watched him finish the final furrows. The tractor bumped and slew as the three plough hooks, weighted by a sack of sand, cut through the volcanic soil, turning out great broken clods and porous rocks. Occasionally, Mahmut stopped, to re-tie his headscarf or drive caked mud from the plough with a metal spike. When the whole field was ploughed, he stood on the tractor stroking his beard, to survey his work. Then he gathered up a jerrycan of water and the remains of his breakfast, before we set off together down the hill to the village, Örencik.

I didn't have to plant wheat, of course. You can make bread from myriad different plants including barley, maize, buckwheat, millet, sorghum and teff, a hardy grass used to make *injera*, the flatbread of choice in Ethiopia. During times of hunger in previous centuries, a wide variety of plant materials including acorns, peas, beans, chestnuts and oats were also ground into flour and used to make rough bread. The main rival to wheat as a bread cereal, though, is rye. I did briefly consider planting rye, when I saw it growing in a neighbour's field in the Black Mountains. Originally a weed of wheat fields, rye was not proactively grown in western Europe until the beginning of the Christian era. Like oats and millet, rye is hardier than wheat, yielding better on poor soils and in adverse climatic conditions. Thus, it was the grain of choice and a key food staple across northern Europe and Russia from at least the medieval period. In parts of eastern Germany, people even called themselves 'Rugii' – the rye eaters. In Britain, rye was often blended with wheat (and other grains and seeds) to make a peasant bread called 'maslin'. When standards of living began to rise in western Europe, at the end of the nineteenth century, brown rye flour fell out of fashion, as wheaten bread prevailed. Rye bread – characteristically dense, dark, earthy and filling – has held its place, however, in the culinary traditions of Scandinavia, the Baltic States and central Europe.

In Germany, a country with a rich bread culture, rye is the pinnacle of popular bread: two of the nation's favourites – *Vollkornbrot* and *Graubrot* – are both made with rye.

Wheat, though, has long been considered the queen of cereals. It is the chief crop of western civilization. From at least the late Middle Ages, wheat has been the grain of choice for making bread for the majority of people in Europe: 'for better bread than ever came from wheat,' Cervantes wrote in *Don Quixote*. Anyone who could afford to live above subsistence preferred it. Foremost, wheat is extremely nutritious, generally containing 60–80 per cent carbohydrates and 8–15 per cent protein. Wheat is also a seasonal crop: intensive labour is required only for sowing and harvesting. This allowed time for the cultivation of other fields, as well as for politicizing and warmongering.

Wherever Europeans have settled, they have planted wheat. Over the course of the nineteenth and twentieth centuries, botanists, engineers and chemists transformed wheat, and thereby the global grain map. Today wheat is unequalled in its range of cultivation; it is planted over an area of 550 million acres worldwide. In 2018–19, the total harvest was some 734 million tonnes. Wheat flour now provides around one fifth of all the calories consumed by humans globally. It is used to make cakes, crackers, cookies, noodles, pastries, pasta, animal feed and more. The cereal gained eminence, though, as a principal ingredient of leavened bread because it contains proteins with distinct properties that cause dough to rise. This results in loaves that are more porous, lighter, finer, tastier and more digestible than bread made with rival cereals.

'One step, one hand,' Mahmut said. We were in another

field, on the other side of the village. Passing his house, Mahmut had stopped to collect a bag of grain and a cotton drape that he tied round his waist and gathered in front of him, creating a bib. With a handful of grain, he cocked his right wrist away from the body and drew his elbow in. As he stepped forward, his forearm sprang forward too, from four o'clock to twelve o'clock, releasing the seed in an immemorial arc. The projected seed was briefly airborne, catching the sunlight in a crescent of tiny crystals before it pattered on the earth. Mahmut stalled momentarily on his straightened right leg while his hand scooped through the bib. Loaded, the hand was cocked again; another crescent of seed shot out. Scatter, step, stall, scoop, step, spring the wrist, scatter, repeat. Mahmut strode across the field to this primal rhythm. This is how everyone sowed wheat until Jethro Tull invented the seed drill in Britain in the eighteenth century, I realized. Mahmut did not aimlessly cast the seed aside, like a child dropping sweet wrappers. Instead, he drove each fistful of grain towards the earth with the purpose of a scything scimitar. For him, sowing wheat was an act of expectation, not of blind hope. His motions connected him directly to the proto-farmers who fed the labourers who erected the megaliths up the hill from his village, at Göbekli Tepe. The synchronicity of advancing feet and the sweeping hand was a dance to the steadfast purpose of man throughout civilization, and a physical invocation of the earth itself, to give abundance.

The rhythm was as natural to Mahmut as it was unnatural to me. With the bib around my waist, I tried to mimic his actions. When I sprang my fist forward, the seed came out in a linear jet rather than an arc. Sometimes, I released my grip too early and scattered the seed behind me. Other times, I forgot to step, and spread two handfuls of seed on the same ground. It was like learning to pat your head and rub your stomach at the same time. When most of the grain was broadcast, Mahmut stopped me and, with a chapped finger, drew a circle in the dirt at our feet. It was, he gesticulated, the size of the palm of his hand. He placed seven grains carefully inside the circle. This was the ideal sowing rate, he explained. On poor soil, you sow a little more, and on good soil, a little less. A fine yield, on volcanic soil, would be thirty grains of wheat for every seed sown. An average return would give you twenty grains.

Tarık arrived and as we ambled back to the village, he translated for his father. Mahmut had not planted anything yet this year, because of the unseasonal heavy rains at the beginning of October. In the next few days, he would meet with five other families and they would plan their communal cereal and vegetable strategy for the growing season, including wheat, barley, oats, aubergines, peppers and lentils. They would begin planting next week. They had tractors now, for ploughing, sowing and harvesting, though Tarık recalled harvesting by hand with sickles as a boy, and Mahmut still owned a sickle.

In the village, children sprang out from behind walls, jiggling and exclaiming 'Good morning, teacher' – their only English words, Tarık explained. Inside the house, a fig tree dominated one side of the baked-mud courtyard and vines ran along the exposed beams. Sultan, Mahmut's wife, looked up from the basket of peppers she was cleaning, shifted her purple headscarf, waved and smiled brightly. The afternoon sun sent long shadows across the courtyard and up the white-washed daub walls. We sat on stools around a low table while Tarık laid out a lunch of bulgur wheat (wholegrains boiled, washed and cooled), onions, goat's cheese, spicy peppers, aubergines and bread.

Bread, or *ekmek* in Turkish, is nearly always made from wheat and it remains the most important foodstuff in the country. In fact, Turkish consumption of bread per capita is one of the highest in the world. The word *ekmek* is even used colloquially for 'livelihood', as in *ekmek kavgasi* (literally 'bread fight'), which means 'struggling to make a living'. On previous visits, I had relished eating *pide* (a flatbread topped with meats and cheeses), *gözleme* (an unleavened, buttered flatbread with different toppings), *pogaca* (a sort of focaccia, usually leavened and often seeded), and *simit* (rings of doughy bread commonly encrusted in sesame seeds and eaten at breakfast), among other varieties. When I cycled across Anatolia during Ramadan in the late 1990s, I sat in restaurants infused with the smell of fresh bread, waiting for the daily fast to end. As the call to evening prayer began, people aching with hunger took a piece of bread, blessed it and raised it to their mouths.

The bread for our lunch was a flatbread made at home by Sultan, which Tarık referred to as 'village bread'. This style of thin, unleavened bread called *yufka* is very similar to *lavash*, and part of an ancient family of flatbreads that are still made in domestic kitchens and communal village bakeries throughout eastern Turkey, Iran, Armenia, Georgia and Azerbaijan. Though *lavash* and *yufka* are made in incrementally different ways across the region, the principles and basic ingredients are the same. There is no easier, no more convenient form of bread, which is why humans have been making *yufka* and *lavash* for thousands of years.

Flour, water and salt are mixed together into a dough, kneaded and left to rest. This dough is an essential component of Turkish cuisine and used in manifold ways from paper-thin *baklava* pastry to savoury *böreks*. Small pieces of dough are then rolled out to semi-transparent thinness in a precise circle with a long, slender, dowel-like rolling pin called an *oklava*. Using an *oklava* requires great dexterity, but it's more than a culinary skill: it is a form of folk art. *Lavash* is baked on the inside wall of a simple mud oven. *Yufka* is generally cooked on top of a domed iron plate or griddle.

Tarık led me into the small kitchen to show me the griddle, called a *saç* in Turkish. In one corner, set in a baked-mud basin beneath a blackened arch, a pot was cooking on a fire of dried animal dung. In the opposite corner, thirty or more *yufka* were piled up on top of each other under a heavy cotton drape. Each round was thin, dry and over a metre in diameter. Tarık explained that his mother bakes once a week, heating the *saç* on animal dung cakes, and makes enough bread for the extended family for seven days. When a *yufka* is required, a sprinkle of water makes the bread soft again. Known as 'winter bread' in mountainous parts of central Anatolia, *yufka* can be stored for up to six months.

Walking back across the courtyard, I asked if Tarık could make *yufka*. He translated the question for his mother and they both smiled – very badly was the answer. Not for the first time, I wondered idly what proportion of home-baked bread is prepared by women every day, worldwide. I have never found a figure based on empirical evidence, but it must be very high.

Mahmut had waited for us, even though he was hungry. Showing a degree of hospitality for which the Kurds are famous, my hosts insisted I begin. The bread was creamy-grey and landscaped with leopard spots, brown dimples and craters where the heat had penetrated the dough. I folded and tore a piece. It was soft, moist and chewy, even though it had been baked three days earlier. We ate eagerly, as the shadows crept across the courtyard. Tarık and Mahmut ensured I had a steady supply of *yufka* on my side of the table. When I had finished, they both implored me to eat more.

'Maybe you make village bread with your wheat,' Tarık said as he swept the table and prepared tea. 'Next year, maybe Mahmut coming your house to eat lunch.'

I felt slightly ridiculous, pouring a bottle of cider into the furrows that Roger had ploughed. It was hardly a scientific alternative to the fertilizers, herbicides and fungicides that modern wheat farmers pour on their fields, to maximize yields. Yet agricultural peoples from around the world, throughout millennia, have offered libations to unseen deities, to protect their fields from frost, flooding, wind, disease and drought. And who am I to doubt them? I only hoped Nick didn't catch me pouring the cider. He had already expressed a mixture of incredulity and mirth at my plan to hand sow emmer wheat: 'Free bird food,' he'd said.

Finding the seed had been difficult enough. I was offered

organic spelt and einkorn by the tonne bag, but nobody in Britain, it seemed, sold emmer. I had one fruitless telephone conversation with a grower in Italy – neither of us understood a word the other said – before I eventually rang a mill in the UK. I knew they sold emmer flour, made from grain sourced in Italy. Without hesitation, they agreed to sell me enough emmer seed to plant half an acre. As soon as it arrived, I did a germination test, to check the seed was fertile. I soaked a hundred seeds in water. After three days, ninety-eight had germinated.

When the cider had drained, I set off down the field with a canvas bag of seed on my hip and Mahmut's instructions in my head, scattering handfuls of grain with dramatic gestures on mother earth. Though the furrows were uneven, the average depth was about right. Sowing small grains like emmer too deep makes it harder for the plants to establish themselves, I'd been told. I was particularly concerned about getting the seed density or plant spacing right – a subject that everyone seemed to have an opinion on. According to contemporary scholars like Columella and Varro, farmers in Roman times planted two bushels (the old-fashioned unit of capacity used for grains and other dry goods, equivalent to around 54kg) per acre. In 1523, John Fitzherbert's *Boke of Husbandry* also advocated sowing two bushels per acre. Many of the agricultural surveys carried out county by county at the beginning of the nineteenth century in Britain recommended a little more seed. Elsewhere, I had read sixteen grains per square foot, 35g per square metre and, for intensively managed modern wheat, thirty-five to forty-five seeds per square foot. Of course, I also had Mahmut's counsel – seven grains in the palm of a hand. I was soon going around in circles with all the information. My confusion was compounded when I read that optimum seeding rates vary with the time of year and method of sowing, while they also differ from one wheat variety to the next, from soil to soil, even from farm to farm. In the end, I decided to follow the simple advice of John Percival in his book *Wheat in Great Britain*, first published in 1934: 'It is profitable policy to be liberal with seed.'

Broadcasting wheat is a meditative, almost mythical activity. I quickly felt islanded from the world. I could have done it all day. Unfortunately, I also had to rake the soil over, to cover up the seeds that had either fallen neatly in the bottom of the furrows, or caught on the small corries, crags and corniches of the broken earth. Driving the tines of the rake into stubborn clods was hard graft. The earth was wet and heavy. After forty-five minutes, I had managed to rake one 10m by 10m square. My lower back was aching and the palms of my hands were red. I thought of God's unforgettable words to Adam, after he has sinned, in Genesis: 'In the sweat of thy face shalt thou eat bread, until thou return to the ground . . . for dust thou art; and unto dust shalt thou return.'

There was intermittent relief from the toil. Each time I looked up, the overlay of clouds had shifted and split again, projecting new flares of sunlight on to the hills, illuminating a single field one time, a winter-grey woodland the next, and then a circle of copper moorland. It started mizzling and I was about to go home when Polly, who runs an excellent local bakery, turned up to put in a shift. When she gave up, having broken her new rake on a hefty clod, I started packing my rucksack up again but my wife and kids arrived to help. With a full team, things suddenly sped up. My eldest daughter, Scarlett, began broadcasting grain with the exuberant gestures of a drum major in a marching band. The rest of us raked in behind her with new vigour.

Even though we might have been figures from a scene played out by every generation of farmers, from the arrival of emmer seed in Britain thousands of years ago until the beginning of the twentieth century, we were more than one passer-by could comprehend. A white van drove very slowly up and down the lane three times, then stopped in the gateway. The driver got out and started photographing us. When my wife and I approached, he blurted out: 'I'm going to call the police. What are your names?' A phone call to Nick settled the stranger's qualms and he went off to bother somebody else. We were still laughing about it when the canvas bag was empty and the last sod had been hauled over its furrow.

To make sense of the myriad species of wheat and their complex classification, I called Dr Ed Dickin. Ed is an authority on cereal production and improvement, and a lecturer at Harper Adams University, a British agricultural college founded in 1901. He also breeds and grows many varieties of wheat in trial plots, both at the university and on his parents' farm in Lincolnshire. On the phone, I explained my plan. Ed thought emmer was a good, 'pretty much bomb-proof' choice. He suggested I complement the emmer by planting a variety of bread wheat – a British 'landrace' wheat perhaps, ideally one that would be resilient to the climate in the Black Mountains.

'That resilience comes at the expense of yield, but you're not strictly interested in yield. You just want wheat that makes tasty bread,' Ed said, when we met in a huge glasshouse at the university. There were growing benches, rows of raised beds, long tables lined by black pots with a multitude of plants, partition walls of glass and a gantry of heaters and hydration systems. In a corner of the glasshouse, Ed showed me the area where he breeds new hybrids of wheat and barley, using historic varieties.

From the beginning of agriculture in the Near East, Ed explained, farmers knew to keep a selection of wheat seeds at harvest-time, to sow for the following year. Over millennia, as each community observed the strongest plants, selected the best ears and re-planted the largest grains, tens of thousands of genetically diverse wheat populations, called 'landraces', evolved across the globe, with the characteristics most likely to thrive in local soils and microclimates. As products of human technology, landrace wheats were dynamic. They adapted to changes in the climate, market forces and even culinary trends. Each population comprised dozens, perhaps hundreds of subtly different varieties of wheat, all with different genotypes. At a practical level, this made landrace populations at least partially resistant to extreme weather and disease, because some of the varieties always yielded – a form of organic insurance for the farmer against total crop failure. As landraces tended to be planted on a small scale, as part of crop rotation systems, they also helped build up soil fertility and even break down the cycle of crop pests and diseases.

By the end of the eighteenth century, there were dozens of different landrace populations in cultivation in Britain alone. They must have been as familiar to farmers as the folk songs they sang in the fields and the movement of the constellations in the night sky. Bakers would have appreciated the complexity and diversity of the flavours and textures of breads made from landrace wheats – the result of deep root systems, abundant leaves and long ripening periods. The nomenclature of land-races was problematic, though, as the farmer-turned-author John Banister noted in his *Synopsis on Husbandry* (1799): 'there is scarcely a market town but has a favourite species, which having been successfully cultivated by some farmer in the neighbourhood, is by him dignified with a pompous title, and becomes the fashionable grain.'

Many of these 'titles', Ed explained, referenced where the landraces were first grown, their characteristic appearance and even the time of year they ripened: 'There is an old land-race called Orange Devon Blue Rough Chaff. The blue-black colour develops on the husks as they ripen. Rough chaff refers to the velvet hairs on the husks and, yep, it's from Devon,' he said. The names of other landrace wheats tripped off his tongue: Kent Old Hoary, Red Lammas, Montgomery Red, April Bearded, Golden Drop and Blue Cone Rivet. They could have been names for hipster craft ales in an East London brewpub.

Until the middle of the nineteenth century, all the wheat grown on the planet would have been landrace populations.

John Letts dates the beginning of the end for landrace wheats in Britain from 1836, and the publication of *On the Varieties, Properties and Classification of Wheat*, written by Sir John Le Couteur, a farmer on the isle of Jersey. In 1882, Scottish plant breeder Patrick Shirreff used hybridization – the deliberate crossing of two plants to create a new hybrid or 'cultivar' that combined the desirable characteristics of both parents – to produce a successful wheat hybrid. The Vilmorin family produced the first modern French wheat a year later. The era of scientific plant breeding had quietly begun. At first, specific lines were selected out of the landraces. Then, single seeds were chosen, hybridized and marketed as distinct varieties, with the aim of cultivating more consistent, higher-yielding wheat. In the early twentieth century, as the search for ideal agronomic qualities intensified, the first commercially successful varieties of wheat were planted by British farmers. Many of these produced poorer-quality grain that could be fed to livestock, for meat production. Meanwhile, wheats with paramount milling and bread-making qualities (including flavour) were often discarded, simply because their yields were lower.

The development of wheat-seed selection and then breeding coincided with the end of a period of upheaval in British agriculture: the consolidation of the Enclosure Acts, the Industrial Revolution and the growth of the British Empire and global trade in general had brought about great change. Under the new agricultural system, every plant in a field was to be the same. The ancient practice of seed-saving by farmers, and of empirical improvements in crops as a result of experimentation by the people who actually grew them, dwindled. The great reservoir of diversity in wheat that had accreted over thousands of years began to drain away. In Britain, the majority of landrace wheats were probably out of cultivation by 1900. A few lingered, though, in the physical and meteorological extremities of Britain, where growing conditions were tougher for the new cultivars.

'We believe the landrace that clung on the longest was actually grown in Wales. It's called Hen Gymro. Maybe you should grow some Hen Gymro,' Ed said.

Hen Gymro (pronounced 'Hen Gum-roh', it means 'Old Welshman') was a well-known landrace wheat in Wales. It was grown across the south-west, a notoriously damp domain facing the Irish Sea, into the 1930s. It was not grown for commercial purposes, but to provide small amounts of locally grown flour for home-baked bread. The Welsh Plant Breeding Station (WPBS), established in 1919 by George Stapleton as a department of what is now Aberystwyth University, with a remit to breed better varieties of farm crops for Wales, started to collect samples of Hen Gymro in the 1920s. The scientists were initially bemused that Welsh farmers determinedly stuck to this old variety, when the nascent seed companies were offering vigorous new cultivars that produced higher yields elsewhere in the British Isles. Investigations soon showed that the farmers' preference was founded on more than ignorance and prejudice, though. Hen Gymro, with over 200 different varieties of wheat in the landrace population, grew better than other varieties on the unfavourable ground in Pembrokeshire, Ceredigion and Carmarthenshire. Crucially, it produced millable grain under adverse ripening conditions. If you have ever been on a summer holiday in south-west Wales, you know what 'adverse ripening conditions' are – wet weather. In addition, the long, slender Hen Gymro straw made excellent thatching material. A 1929 WPBS report concluded that Hen Gymro should 'maintain its popularity where small areas are grown for household purposes'. Even though I live in south-east Wales, it sounded perfect. A smile flicked across Ed's face: 'You're in luck. I happen to have a bag of Hen Gymro seed here. It's yours.'

Actually, the seed Ed proposed to give me was even more esoteric. As we walked back through the glasshouse, he explained how plant breeders at WPBS had selected and briefly bred several strains or 'pure lines' of the landrace in the 1920s, in an effort to improve Hen Gymro for small-scale growers in Wales. One of these strains, prosaically named S.72, was briefly marketed in 1928. The drive to improve agricultural production in Britain, prior to and particularly during the Second World War, was killing off the last of the landrace wheats fast, though. In some instances, seeds from landrace populations were saved by botanists and housed in early seed banks. Many ancient landrace varieties, however, simply vanished. Seeds from the original Hen Gymro line were collected and saved in British gene banks. The S.72 line was lost.

'At least we thought it was lost,' Ed said. 'But it turned out that a sample of Hen Gymro S.72 seeds *was* saved, in a seed bank in Russia called the Vavilov Institute.' The N. I. Vavilov All-Russian Scientific Research Institute of Plant Industry in St Petersburg is named after one of the outstanding scientists of the twentieth century, and perhaps the greatest wheat collector of all time. Nicolai Ivanovich Vavilov (1887–1943) was a botanist, geneticist and plant explorer possessed with that rare and excellent combination of traits – great intellect, inexhaustible energy and military efficiency. In the face of seismic changes in agriculture in the early twentieth century, Vavilov understood the urgent need to conserve genetic variation in plants through intensive collecting, research and preservation, to provide food security in the future: 'Every single packet of grain, every handful of seeds and every bundle of ripe spikelets is of the utmost scientific value,' he wrote. He set about establishing a global seed bank – a collection of plants that would, one day, offer 'the possibility . . . by means of crossing, to synthesize forms such as are absolutely unknown in nature'.

The son of a prosperous Moscow merchant, who had himself grown up in a Russian village haunted by crop failures and the threat of starvation, Vavilov became obsessed as a young man with the role that science could play in ending famine. He devoted himself to collecting the seeds of landrace plants, as well as their wild relatives, from across the planet. Between 1916 and 1941, he undertook expeditions on five continents, to sixty-four countries. It is thought that he collected more seeds, tubers and fruits from species and strains of wild and cultivated plants – some 220,000 – than any other person in history. He also developed a theory on the origins of the most important crops, published in 1926 as 'Centres of Origins of Cultivated Plants', which remains influential among botanists today.

Vavilov understood that the landrace wheats he was collecting were 'the result of intelligent, innovative minds – and often the work of geniuses,' as he wrote. These 'geniuses' were traditional peasant farmers working with nature. At the scientific institute Vavilov headed under Lenin's patronage, he devised a comprehensive system for evaluating, studying and utilizing his own 'introductions', plus those gathered by other collectors. In the early 1930s, it was the largest seed bank on earth. The collection contained over 100,000 wheat samples, including a small amount of Hen Gymro S.72.

Like many Soviet scientists, Vavilov eventually fell foul of Joseph Stalin during the period of political repression known as 'the Great Terror'. The dictator needed a scapegoat: his agricultural collectivization programmes had failed, leading to crop failures and mass famine. An estimated four million Ukrainians died of starvation during the 'Holodomor' famine in 1932–3. Stalin also disapproved of the plant collector's un-Soviet ideas on genetics, his endless expeditions, and the circle of international scientists Vavilov moved among. In August 1940, as the Second World War rolled towards the Soviet Union, a KGB car picked Vavilov up while he was on yet another plant-collecting trip, in the Ukraine. He never saw his wife and son again. He was interrogated, tortured and sentenced to death for defending the 'bourgeois pseudo-science' of genetics. In 1943, one of the world's foremost authorities on plants, and arguably the individual who did more than any other in the first half of the twentieth century to provide humankind with plentiful food, died of starvation in a gulag – a grim irony, no doubt lost on Stalin.

There is an extraordinary postscript. During the 872-day Siege of Stalingrad in the Second World War, scientists and curators at the institute Vavilov had built up locked themselves into the neoclassical building on St Isaac's Square, in the city centre. They were determined to protect the vault of seeds both from their own starving people and from the Nazis, who not only knew about the collection, but had established a commando unit to seize it. Staff at the institute boxed up a cross-section of the seeds, moved them to the basement and guarded them round the clock. In a display of heroic devotion – to Vavilov, their inspirational leader for a long time, to the future of food security in the Soviet Union, and to the genetic diversity and health of plant species on earth – they refused to eat a single seed from this remarkable trove, even when the pangs of hunger tormented them, day after day. A dozen of them starved to death at their desks.

In a final twist as black as the Ukrainian soil, Vavilov's death sentence was posthumously reversed in 1955. The storied institute that he ran for nineteen years was named after him in 1968. It still holds one of the largest collections of plant genetic material on earth, albeit in a slightly chaotic, under-funded, post-Soviet fashion. Several years ago, Andy Forbes contacted the Vavilov Institute. Andy is, among his many roles, a 'wheat chaser' who has saved several ancient varieties from extinction. In 2014, Andrew Whitley visited St Petersburg to bring small samples of several wheats back to the British Isles, including an envelope containing a handful of Hen Gymro S.72 seeds. These seeds were sown in trial plots in the UK, to increase the volume of grain over successive years. There is now enough of the S.72 strain to be planted in small field strips, Ed explained, handing me the sack of grain.

Modern varieties of wheat that are bred and sold by private seed companies to be sown on a vast scale, coated in chemicals and milled into flour for industrial-scale bakeries, don't grow well under organic farming practices. In the absence of any commercial imperative, the same seed companies have failed to develop niche varieties of wheat that would do well for organic farmers. The new wave of organic bakers, however, have created a small market that is driving a resurgence of interest in landrace wheats. As well as bulking up the different lines of Hen Gymro, Ed was also planting out, studying and selecting several other landraces, and even crossing them with modern varieties, in the search for a high-yielding wheat that makes nutritious, tasty bread. He had trial plots of Red Lammas, Old Kent Red, einkorn, Mulika Holdfast cross, a Georgian wheat called Tsiteli Doli and other varieties, as well as barley, all growing on the university farm.

'Landrace wheats have several natural advantages. Because the plants grow tall, they tend to out-compete and suppress weeds. They have larger root systems than modern varieties, which support more mycorrhizae of fungi in the soil, and they are more resistant to diseases like septoria, rust and powdery mildew. I think you'll find the Hen Gymro is pretty robust,' Ed said, lifting the bag of grain into the boot of my car. He pursed his lips, raised his eyebrows and looked at me keenly. I decoded this into a succinct parting message – Don't screw up.

Shaking hands, I asked him about the ideal weather for growing wheat. He rubbed his chin. Not too cold or wet through winter, he said, as waterlogging stops the root system growing, and even kills the plants. Plenty of rain in May and June, then at least three warm, dry, bright weeks for the grain to ripen properly before harvest: 'Not much to ask for,' he concluded.

Come wind, come weather, I thought. And it did. Driving home, the rain hammered down. The next day, it rained harder still. The day after that, it fell first in buckets, then in sheets, and finally in charcoal slabs. Still the rain came, contemptuously. In fact, it rained every day for five weeks. The River Usk burst its banks. My acre flooded. A brown pond formed in a depression across the middle of the plot, submerging a circle of the emmer that had initially germinated and established itself so well. The chain of low-pressure systems barrelling off the Atlantic and into the hills of Wales finally broke on 20 January. The sky had rained itself out. I rang Ed to ask if it was too late in the season to plant Hen Gymro. He said the cut-off point was the end of the month.

A week later, when the field had dried out, my friend Slim came down the hill in his old Massey Ferguson tractor. He tilled the soil, planted the Hen Gymro seed and harrowed it over, in under two hours. As Slim chugged off back up the hill, I walked around my blessèd plot again. I thought of the seed in the ground, silently absorbing moisture and sequestering warmth, to activate the enzymes that trigger growth. The earth abides. Just. I had managed to get two thirds of an acre of wheat sown in time. The surface of the soil, gilded by the declining sun, was almost smooth. There was a sense of calm, a sense of an ending. I luxuriated in that for a moment, even though I knew that my labours to make bread from seed had barely begun.

CHAPTER 2

As Ye Sow, So Shall Ye Reap: Harvesting

'And he gave it for his opinion, that whoever could make
two ears of corn, or two blades of grass, to grow upon a
spot of ground where only one grew before, would deserve
better of mankind, and do more essential service to his
country, than the whole race of politicians put together.'
— Jonathan Swift, *Gulliver's Travels*

The complex world of domesticated wheat can be roughly
divided into spring and winter varieties. Spring wheat is
planted, as the name suggests, in spring and harvested in late
summer. It grows continuously and generally produces grain
with a high protein content. Spring wheats are favoured in
northernmost latitudes, where the earth is iron-hard during
winter. Winter wheat is planted in autumn or early winter and
harvested in early summer. Most British wheats are winter
varieties, for several reasons. The longer a plant is in the
ground the better it develops, particularly in our climate. Also,
oats and barley were traditionally sown in spring, leaving a
window in autumn for farmers to sow wheat. Critically, winter
wheat must 'vernalize' in cold temperatures. After it has germinated and emerged from the earth, the plants then need to
be dormant, showing no growth or change for four to eight

weeks, depending on the variety. This period of dormancy prevents them from developing too soon, risking frost damage to the ears. Once it has vernalized, winter wheat is able to recognize the signal of longer days, which triggers the flowering process and the production of seed. If winter wheat fails to vernalize, it carries on growing in a simple, vegetative state, producing more and more leaves but little or no grain: 'You end up with a big lawn to mow,' Ed Dickin had told me. Confusingly, emmer is neither a winter wheat nor a spring wheat. It is 'facultative', which means it does not have a vernalization requirement and can be planted in autumn or spring. Hen Gymro, however, is a winter wheat: it has to vernalize. The fact that I had planted my Hen Gymro seed so late, in mild weather, was a concern. I needed winter to fasten its frigid grip.

February was, thankfully, cold. At the end of the month, a storm called the 'Beast from the East' brought a blast of hard, Siberian weather to the whole country. My field was framed by truncated, white hills and corrugated with crusted ripples of ice; it looked like a woodcut print. On 1 March, the first day of spring according to meteorologists, more snow fell, deadening the land. Britain came to a standstill. Schools closed, trains and flights were cancelled, motorways were blocked and thousands of homes were without power. Army helicopters were deployed to drop supplies to farmers and hermits in the frosted hills. And I was happy – briefly.

The 'Great Waiting', as farmers used to call winter, then refused to relent. Day after day I returned to the field, looking for the immemorial stirrings of spring. My wife said it was like watching the toaster – the more I stood in the field, the longer it would take for spring to come. She was right, but I still stood in the field. I was now anxious to know if my wheat would 'tiller', the physiological process by which a single seedling can produce multiple stems or tillers, all of which may produce grains. I read that in ideal circumstances, in well-cultivated, well-drained soils with no weeds, good tilth and ample root space, a single grain of a landrace wheat can produce forty, fifty or even a hundred tillers, resulting in thousands of grains. That was highly unlikely to happen in my field, not least because of the heavy rains in early winter, but I grasped the point: tillering is the route to abundance.

Though farmers have some control over the cultivation and manuring of the land, over the choice of plants and the sowing of the seed, over the cocktail of chemicals used to treat the plants, if that is the chosen route, and over the general management of crops during growth, they cannot control the temperature, the rainfall and the amount of sunshine. The weather, often of the greatest importance, is out of the grower's hands. Standing in my field on the day spring did finally arrive, it struck me – planting wheat remains a horticultural act of faith.

On Rogation Sunday in April, I went to the Church of St Issui at Patricio, deep in the Black Mountains, to pray for a bountiful harvest. The church is one of the most picturesque places of worship in Britain. Daffodils lit up the graveyard. Above the church, the elixir of spring sunshine was raising the moors from heavy winter sedation. I'm not religious and I wasn't sure who I was praying to, but I needed help from somewhere. The snow had cleared on my acre to reveal a large circle of barren earth, where waterlogging had killed off some of my emmer plants. There was also an empty semi-circle along the fence, where rabbits and crows had pulled up my Hen Gymro seedlings. By this point, I couldn't get an old country rhyme out of my head: 'Sow four grains in a row / One for the pigeon, one for the crow / One to rot, and one to grow.' I wasn't even sure if one in four of the seeds I had sown were now going to make it.

Historically, Rogation – from the Latin *rogare*, meaning 'to ask' – was a period of fasting and abstinence between Easter and Ascension, during which the Church offered prayers for God's blessing on the fertility of the earth. The Christian Rogation festival replaced an annual Roman pagan procession, the Robigalia, organized to propitiate the deity of agricultural diseases and, specifically, to protect wheat fields. No doubt, asking some supramundane entity for decent weather and a good harvest goes back even further than Roman times, possibly all the way back to the beginning of farming itself.

On the cover of the church service sheet, there was an illustration of a farmer carrying a sheaf of wheat from the fields. During the Collect, the vicar asked God to 'bless the labours of those who work on land . . . and grant us good harvest'. In the reading from Deuteronomy, we heard: 'For the Lord your God is bringing you into a good land . . . a land of wheat and barley, of vines and fig trees and pomegranates . . . a land where you may eat bread without scarcity.' As we listened to the sermon, prayed and occasionally exclaimed 'Alleluia', the door to the church was open. A tongue of sunlight lit up the flagstone floor and birdsong mingled with the organ as we lustily sang, 'We plough the fields and scatter the good seed on the land.'

Reflecting on this, I felt a weight lift. I had been anxious about my wheat for months, about how it was growing and what yield I would get. In worrying about tiller numbers, stand density and kernel size, I had fallen too easily for the Abrahamic conception of land as a commodity belonging to us, from which we should extract the highest yield at any cost. I thought of Aldo Leopold, the early American environmentalist, who wrote: 'When we see land as a community to which we belong, we may begin to use it with love and respect.' I should have been looking for a different kind of harvest all along, a harvest that could be measured in aesthetic, emotional and familial terms, not in weight of grain. After all, the word 'cultivate', which comes from the Medieval Latin *cultivare*, meaning 'to till, to care for plants', also means to civilize or refine one's mind or manners. 'In harvest teach,' William Blake wrote.

I went back to my field with a lighter heart. I now saw the abundant seedlings that were growing, rather than the blank earth where they were not. I lay down in the field and napped on sunny afternoons. Sometimes, I read poetry out loud to the wheat. Having read about the power of music on plants, I took a speaker and played Beethoven, the Ramones and Gil Scott-Heron, all the time desperately hoping Nick the farmer wouldn't turn up. His wheat looked spectacularly healthy, without even a blast from the Ramones. I even went to the field at night, under clear skies, to find Virgo, the largest constellation of the Zodiac that is visible in the northern hemisphere from mid-March to the end of June. The 'winged maiden' has been associated with fertility and agriculture since antiquity. The Romans saw the goddess of agriculture and fertility, Ceres – whence we get the word 'cereal' – in Virgo's shape, while the Greeks saw Demeter, goddess of the harvest and one of their best-loved deities. Earlier still the Babylonians associated the constellation with their own grain-goddess, Astarte. At first, I could not find this rambling group of stars. Then I identified Spica, by star-hopping from the handle of the Big Dipper asterism. Spica, Latin for 'ear of grain', is one of the brightest stars in the sky. Lying on my back, letting the warm night air wash over me, I let my eye walk lazily from Spica over the phalanx of stars until, eventually, the pattern emerged. There was Virgo, the winged harvest-goddess, holding her sheaf of wheat, radiating down upon me.

By the end of April, spring was effulgent and things were happening fast in the field. Every few days, there was something new to observe. Tillers formed, leaves followed. The emmer stalks began to form nodes and telescope upwards. Soon the ears or heads were clearly visible inside the flag leaf sheaths, on the stalks. The weather was sensational. It was so hot that my kids insisted we went swimming in the River Usk, night after night. During the first week in May, the emmer heads emerged, armoured with elegant, long whiskers called 'awns'. Anthers then appeared on the heads: flowering had begun. It was a moment of glee. Pollination and fertilization would follow. There would, at least, be some grain to harvest come the summer.

*

Mohammed Abdul Rahman Maliji closed the palms of his hands, enveloping the seed head. He rubbed in a circular motion for a few seconds. Flecks of desiccated awns broke off and fell to the earth. When he opened his hands, the perfect seed head of wheat had been crushed to a matchbox-size heap. Cupping his hands, he blew sharply through pursed lips, as if putting a candle out. A hundred pieces of chaff took flight. Momentarily, they formed a speckled balloon between us. Mohammed tipped the remnants back and forth between his palms, disturbing the remaining flakes with more short breaths. When all the chaff was gone, he held up a flattened palm for me to inspect. Two dozen golden-brown pearls of wheat had gathered along the deepest palmar creases. Here was sunlight brought down to earth and converted into essential human sustenance. By feeling and then biting into the kernels, Mohammed explained, he knew if the wheat was ready to harvest. When I nodded, he raised his open palm again and with a snap of the wrist, shot the berries into his mouth. Laughing and chewing, he picked up another seed head and beckoned me to have a go.

We were in a field of wheat near the village of Rushdie, five kilometres from the city of Faqus, and a hundred kilometres north-east of Cairo, in Sharqia Province, the most important wheat-growing region in Egypt for millennia. The main course of the Nile is eighty kilometres west of Rushdie, but the extensive network of subsidiary channels and irrigation canals ensure Mohammed's fields are watered by the world's longest river, as they were in ancient times. Then, the Bubastite branch of the Nile flowed nearby. We know this because King

Ramses II, whose long reign in 1279–1213 BC marked the last great peak of Egypt's imperial power, built a palace on this site, and moved his capital here. There were storehouses, administrators' residences, docks on the river and great temples. Before that, the same rich agricultural riverine land was home to the Hyksos. This ethnic group, thought to be from Palestine originally, ruled northern Egypt c.1630–1523 BC, from a prominent settlement called Avaris, which also encompassed the fields where Mohammed and I stood. Earlier still, the site was a town during the Middle Kingdom, 1938–1630 BC. Mohammed pointed to the large white villa with faded green wooden shutters fifty metres away. It belonged to the Austrian Archaeological Institute, he said, though nobody comes to carry out excavations any more.

Getting out of Cairo, a polyglot megacity with a metropolitan population of over twenty million, was not easy. Ahmed Hamed, a friend and I rode the metro to the end of the line, in the grim, grey suburbs. From there we took a microbus past wheel-hub shops, unfinished concrete flyovers and roadside butchers selling camel meat, towards Faqus. For mile after diesel-choked mile, the road, which followed a canal, was lined with half-built blocks of new flats. Finally, Cairo, 'the city of a thousand minarets', worn to a thread and exhausted, gave way. We then sped by banana plantations, groves of palm trees, fields of aubergines, egrets and live camels. Everywhere, the wheat harvest was in full flow. In some fields, teams worked with sickles. In others, threshing machines were disgorging cascades of chaff into the air. Great bales of straw were being carried to the roadside on donkey carts and sacks of grain were being humped on to lorries by bull-necked men. There were hundreds of people in these fields. I thought about harvest-time at home, and the sight of a lone tractor-driver in a sea of gold.

In Faqus, Ahmed Ajami swept us away from the turmoil of the central bus station. I was keen to get to the village, but Ahmed's father, a producer of honey and olive oil on his organic farm in Sinai, had arranged lunch. We drank black, sweet, strong and refreshing tea before a great tray of food arrived. There were olives, hard-boiled eggs, chillies, honey, cream and cheeses. Two varieties of bread had been prepared for me: *Aish merahrah mladen* is a crisp, round flatbread made with maize flour and ground fenugreek seeds. It is prepared in village homes in the Nile Delta. Because it is baked dry, these great rounds, almost one metre in diameter, remain edible for weeks. The other type of bread, *Feteer mshaltet*, a pastry-like bread cooked with wheat flour, salt, sugar, water and ghee, is traditionally made for guests in rural Egypt and is a symbol of hospitality. In the cities, *feteer* is a street-food made with a variety of sweet and savoury toppings or fillings.

We ripped and snapped the breads apart, turning morsels into utensils to scoop slivers of cheese and dab dollops of honey. Ahmed's father told me that the *feteer* was made with flour from a historic variety of wheat that he grows for the family to eat, but not to sell. It is low-yielding, compared to the modern varieties of bread wheat which the vast majority of farmers in Egypt now plant, but it has more flavour. Agriculture, he said, has been the main economic activity in Upper

Egypt since the time of the pharaohs. Today, cucumbers, potatoes, oranges, peaches, apricots, peanuts, maize, rice and wheat, which remains the main winter cereal crop throughout the country, are all grown in abundance. Bread wheat is planted in November and the harvest this year was almost finished. It had been an acceptable harvest, though the yield was 20 per cent down on the previous year, because of a heat-wave earlier in April. When it is too hot, the seeds do not plump up sufficiently.

When we had finished lunch, there was another round of tea and cigarettes before Ahmed's father declared the best time to harvest was when the sun is high. With multiple hand-shakes and profuse expressions of goodwill, we were then bustled out into the car for the drive along the canal to the village. When we arrived, Mohammed, forty-five years old and slim, with a crown of boot-polish black hair, heavy eye-brows, glasses and a thin moustache, was cutting wheat barefoot. Two teenagers were helping – his son, Sa'id, and his nephew, also called Mohammed. The field belonged to his aunt, but he farmed it for her. In fact, he farms for several members of his family and has to harvest eight 'kirats', an ancient Egyptian unit of land equivalent to 175 square metres. One of the defining characteristics of Egyptian agriculture today is the prevalence of small-scale, household farms where wheat is grown in small plots and mainly consumed for sub-sistence. Mohammed has been a farmer all his life. He learnt how to harvest with his grandfather, which is important, he stressed – you feel a connection to the family in the fields at this time of year. On a good day, he could harvest and stack one kirat of wheat by hand himself, but with the help of other family members, the harvest is usually completed in four days.

We stepped over the neatly cinched bundles of cut wheat lying in the field and walked up a mound, to the village grave-yard. In every direction there were fields of wheat and stubble divided by culverts, dykes, spillways and sluices that brought water from the river. In a field nearer the village, a corps of women and children from several families were busily feeding wheat into a threshing machine, powered by a fanbelt off the back of a tractor.

Walking back, I asked Mohammed about the women. Yes, of course, women were involved in wheat production, par-ticularly at harvest-time, he explained. The women in his family would ordinarily help him, but as I was here, Islamic modesty meant they stayed home. I had read that women make up over 40 per cent of the agricultural labour force, on average, across developing countries. It struck me as likely that this has been the case in Sharqia Province since the emer-gence of agriculture, millennia ago. Yet, finding women farmers in the economic history books I had been reading was remarkably hard. This could be because of the male-biased view of agricultural historians, or it could be on account of the laws and traditions that barred women from owning and inheriting land in many cultures. Either way, women have been essential but silent contributors in farming, throughout history. Ahmed Hamed translated something I had read – 'If you teach a man to farm, his family will eat. If you teach a woman to farm, the community will eat' – and both he and Mohammed nodded slowly.

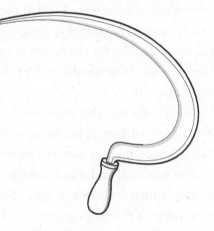

Handing me a sickle, Mohammed explained why he still refused to harvest with a machine, even though many of his neighbours now did: 'The machines cut the straw too high above the ground. They also spill a lot of seed. Perhaps, if we owned a larger piece of land, it would be possible to harvest with a machine, but our plots are small and we can't afford the waste. Also, you need to feel the harvest,' he said.

Sinking down on his haunches with lithesome ease, Mohammed started cutting. I rolled the hardwood handle of the sickle across my palm. The rough steel blade was 25cm long and 3cm at its maximum width, tapering to a sharp tip. I estimated the blade concavity to be no more than 6 or 7cm. I thought of a sickle moon in the night sky, and I wondered if this was the original inspiration for the shape. The angle of the blade with the handle was perhaps 10 degrees. Dozens of 2mm-long, serrated teeth had been filed into the steel cutting edge, at an angle of around 60 degrees with the blade, so they shaped down towards the handle. I rolled the sickle in my hand again and guessed the weight – 250 grams. I rocked it gently up and down, feeling for the centre of gravity. Then I closed my fingers round the handle and let the sickle hang from the end of my arm.

It is hard to think of a tool that has been more important, not just in the history of Egypt, but in the entire history of bread. The Natufians commonly used composite sickles comprising tooth-like obsidian and flint bladelets inserted with cypress resin into animal jawbones or wood handles for harvesting plants. Many of the large quantities of sickle blades that have been found in archaeological digs across the Near East are 'glossed' or covered in a silica patina that suggests they were used for cutting cereals. The intricacy of their design and the manufacturing sophistication comparative to other tools suggest they were critical to the first farmers in the Fertile Crescent. By the time of the Neolithic Revolution and the domestication of wheat, the sickle would have felt like an extension of the hand to a proto-farmer, just as it did to me, even though I had never used one before.

Between the dawn of the Iron Age in Anatolia, around the beginning of the first millennium BC, and the present, thousands of regional and even plant-specific variants of this basic tool have been developed, forged of iron and then steel. Their cutting edges, however, fall into just two distinct styles or patterns – smooth or serrated. While both can be used for cutting green grasses or mature cereals, the serrated sickle has long been favoured for harvesting wheat. And even though the scythe, basically a sickle on a long handle that was known to the Romans and first became popular in eighth-century Europe, offered greater efficiency in certain circumstances, the sickle remains a go-to tool today for tens of millions of farmers in Asia, Africa, the Middle East, Central and South America, and even in mountainous parts of southern Europe. The universal nature and symbolism of the sickle was crystallized by Lenin in 1917, when, crossed with a hammer and set in a wreath of wheat, it became the first state emblem of the Soviet Union.

Mohammed raised his sickle towards me and touched his thumb against the rough teeth of the blade: 'The sickle is sharpened once a year, before harvest,' he said. I thought of my scythe at home. When I am mowing grass, I sharpen it every fifteen minutes. Mohammed then stretched his arms out in front of him and, with the sickle in his right hand, he hooked a dozen stalks of wheat. As the left hand caught the stalks, he made a short, deft cut towards him with his right hand. He repeated the process and the sickle flickered blue and silver through the wheat, like a spooked trout darting across a sunlit stream. When his left hand was full with thirty or so stalks, he reached out to the side and placed the bunch on the earth. Watching more closely, I realized Mohammed was not actually cutting the straw – he was sawing it, with the serrated teeth. As farmers under the pharaohs knew, if you hit the wheat stalks, the grains are more likely to fall to the ground; if you saw gently, the grains hold in the ears, ready to be threshed at the appropriate time. The further apparent advantage of the sickle over the scythe was the free hand, which is used to gather and place the cut stalks in neat piles.

Mohammed gesticulated for me to begin alongside him. I

spat on my hand and grasped the sickle. Sa'id watched me carefully. He motioned when I was getting it wrong, and signalled ways to improve. After ten minutes, I fell into a rhythm. After twenty minutes, I was hypnotized. I even forgot about the pain in my knees. It struck me as incredible that people have been harvesting wheat to make bread in exactly this fashion, plausibly in this field, every April, for 6,000 years. What did that mean for a fourteen-year-old boy like Sa'id, I wondered. Was the connection to his distant ancestors through this refined physical act something he considered or even felt? Did this remarkable continuity in human experience somehow give him purpose? I did try to enquire. I asked Ahmed Hamed if he could translate my questions. Ahmed looked at me benignly and shrugged, then he wandered off to photograph a boy jiggling past on a donkey.

When we paused for a slug of tea from Mohammed's flask, I measured our progress. Four of us had cut the area of half a tennis court in an hour. The wheat lay in neat piles behind us. Harvesting by hand, Mohammed explained, was easier and more efficient if the planting rate was right. There were some weeds that would have to be removed before the piles were bound, and a few stalks of wild oats. Mohammed also pulled out a rogue stem of barley, to show me how it differed from wheat in the shape of the ear and the pattern of the awns. The wheat, he explained, was a bit green still, but it would continue to ripen for a few more days in bundles, in the field. Though this was not a particularly good harvest, Mohammed hoped to get nearly one 'ardeb' – the traditional unit for measuring cereal crops in Egypt and equal to 150kg – per kirat. I was amazed. Even using these traditional, small-scale cultivation methods, he expected to get the equivalent of 3.6 tonnes of wheat per acre. The wheat would be threshed here in the field, using a machine. Some of the grain would be sold on the spot, to a commercial miller in Faqus. The rest would be transported across the fields to the village and stored at home. The straw would be fed to Mohammed's animals. Eight kirats produced straw to feed two oxen for six months.

Yields of wheat in Egypt have been legendary from the moment agriculture reached the Nile valley, around 6,500 years ago. By the end of the fourth millennium BC, when the historical period dawned with the unification of Upper and Lower Egypt and the First Dynasty of the pharaohs, high yields were assured. In Roman times, when Egypt supplied a third of the Eternal City's grain, yields were estimated to be ten to twenty-seven times higher than the amount sown. Later still, in 1798, the team of scholars appointed by Napoleon Bonaparte to survey Egypt reported that crop yields exceeded those in western Europe. These outstanding yields were a product of the rich, alluvial black earth deposited on an area of 19,000 square kilometres when the Nile flooded every year. 'The gift', as Herodotus called the flood, comprised soil brought by the Blue Nile from the volcanic Highlands of Ethiopia, mixed with organic matter from the swampy sources of the White Nile. The persistence and the clock-like regularity of the river's rhythms – the majestic, unvarying annual cycle known as 'Akhet' or 'Inundation', 'Peret' or 'Coming forth', and 'Shemu' or 'Harvest' – encouraged the intensification and ritualization of agricultural practices.

Regular harvests, high yields and, crucially, a surplus of storable foods – principally dried cereals, which have strong natural defensive systems that ensure the grain does not spoil – transformed the nature of human existence in ancient Egypt. Food was wealth and the seed stores were Egypt's real gold. The phenomenon of food production, out of a benign earth that replenished itself with Nile silt, conditioned social patterns, religion and the thinking of ancient Egyptians. They understood that civilization, with its diversified human activities, arts and architecture, was the fruit of cultivating the soil. The annual harvest, in time, fostered the idea that life was eternal; this led to the building of structures in which the dead bodies of the most powerful people could await reunion with their souls.

We know about grain agriculture in Egypt because the burial chambers or tombs of the hegemony were furnished not just with comforts and treasures for the afterlife, but also with depictions of contemporary activities. Thus, we can study the annual cycle of wheat and the production of bread in almost cinematic detail. In the Tomb of Ti at Saqqara, the vast burial ground near the ancient capital of Memphis, mural reliefs dating from around 2600 BC depict planting, harvesting, threshing, grain storage, grinding, kneading, baking and even the delivery of bread to the office of the estate, where it is received in the presence of a kneeling priest. Fragments from mural paintings that, in the early 18th Dynasty, decorated a tomb within the civil necropolis at Thebes, and which now hang in the Louvre, Paris, show even more detail: farmers dressed in loincloths hoe, plough, broadcast seed and cut the ears with sickles, while women glean the fields, and wheat is threshed beneath the hooves of oxen.

The Greeks called the Egyptians *artophagoi* or 'the bread eaters'. Everyone ate bread at every meal, irrespective of social class, from the pharaohs who had loaves placed in their funerary tombs, to the labourers building the pyramids, whose wages were paid in beer (made from barley), onions and emmer bread. It is even thought that the first leavened bread – 'the most important event in the history of grains,' according to H. E. Jacobs in *Six Thousand Years of Bread* – came from Egypt. In fact, through manipulating yeast in dough, using bread moulds and baking in closed ovens, the Egyptians developed a system of bread making that, in essence, we still use today.

Because of the arid climate, a large number of ancient Egyptian loaves have survived the intervening millennia. Today, several hundred specimens, mostly from funerary offerings, are housed in museum collections throughout the world. These loaves, made from grains that were harvested under the pharaohs, vary widely. In texture, they range from mealy to fine. Some contain cracked, cooked grains, like a modern multigrain bread; others are flavoured with coriander seeds, poppy seeds and herbs; yet more are sweetened with honey or dried fruits like figs and dates. They come in many different shapes and sizes, from cylindrical cones, braided breads, three-cornered discs and fans, to fish, animal and even basic human figures. There are more bread artefacts from ancient Egypt than any other period up to modern times. Bread has even been found in the stomach of mummified remains.

We have a wealth of information about how these loaves were created too. Relief paintings, hieroglyphic texts, pottery, models of bakeries (placed in tombs to offer services to the deceased) and excavations of actual bakeries reveal much about the bread-making process in Egypt. A wooden model of a bakery was found in the tomb of Meketre, near Thebes, in 1920. Dating from *c.*1981–1975 BC, the model gives the sense of a bustling bakery and illustrates the entire process in detail.

In Egypt today, bread is called *aish* rather than *khobz*, the word used by the rest of the Arabic world. *Aish* literally means 'life', which reflects the importance of bread in Egyptian culture. Bread is hardwired into the collective consciousness and fundamental to the national diet, just as it would have been in Europe up to the beginning of the twentieth century. In fact, Egyptians are among the largest consumers of bread by volume in the world today. The simple, round, doughy pockets of pitta-like bread called *aish baladi* are consumed with almost every meal and, in the cities, ubiquitous. Walking round the centre of Cairo with Ahmed Hamed the day before visiting the Nile Delta, there seemed to be a wooden cart peddling *aish baladi* on every second street corner. In the narrow defiles of the Old City, bicycle-delivery boys rode past us, balancing trays of breads on their heads.

In a bakery near Bab al Futuh, one of the gates in the medieval walls of the Old City, I watched *aish baladi* being made. The dough – wholemeal flour, water, dried yeast and salt – was mixed in a great aluminium vat with a mechanical prong. It was then transferred to a wooden bath tub that was coated with a grey patina and left to rise for fifteen minutes. One of the dozen employees with heavily floured hands then deftly scooped out tennis ball-sized blobs of dough and dropped them on to a wooden tray coated in bran. The blobs, ten to each tray, spread out into creamy saucers. At the next station, another baker caressed the dough with the palms of his hands and then gently chopped each saucer like a masseur loosening a knot of muscle. There was a dynamic choreography to the whole routine and an energy, which I had clearly interrupted. In the restricted space, I was in the way all the time.

The trays were stacked next to the brick oven, which glowed red. The senior baker, a grey-haired man in a Hawaiian shirt with a pirate's smile, transferred each dough circle, now 20cm in diameter, to a 'peel', a flat, wooden paddle-like baker's implement. With great dexterity, he made each one hop on his fingers until he could place it precisely on the oblong blade. When there were five in a line, he ran the two-metre handle of the peel through his hands and with a flourish, like the flick of a fly fisherman's wrist, he unloaded the dough on to the oven floor and withdrew the peel. Staring into the oven – and getting in everyone's way again – I watched the flaccid saucers rise spectacularly from the oven floor and grow into plump, tanned puffs that hummed with heat and life. The breads were cooked in thirty seconds. With an even greater display of manual finesse, the baker ran the peel inside the red maws again and somehow loaded five breads back on to the paddle. Too hot to touch, the breads were flicked on to a rattan frame and carried to the front of the bakery, where they were stacked on motorized tuk-tuks and bicycles, to be distributed to

subsidizing staple foods, including bread in the form of *aish baladi*, at the end of the Second World War. When Gamal Abdel Nasser and his military allies staged a coup d'état and overthrew the monarchy in 1952, the authoritarian government continued to use cheap bread to maintain order, while promoting a socialist economic model.

Of course, there is nothing new in state-subsidized food. In ancient Rome, as in modern Egypt, bread was the most important item in people's diet. In 123 BC, the Roman government instituted the regular distribution of free or subsidized grain, acknowledging that any movement in the price of imported wheat had political consequences. In 46 BC, Julius Caesar learnt that 320,000 residents were receiving grain gratis, out of a total free population of 600,000. As the satirist Juvenal quipped, *panem et circenses* ('bread and circuses') played a crucial role in the Roman leadership's strategy on keeping order among a restive, urban citizenry. By the third century AD, the dole of grain was replaced with free bread. Shakespeare based his play *Coriolanus* on an event in early Republican Rome, in which the government was forced to distribute free grain when the people rioted (though he was almost certainly referencing bread riots that took place, as part of a wider plebeian uprising, in England, in 1607): 'The gods know I speak this in hunger for bread, not in thirst for revenge,' a mutinous citizen says in the opening scene of the play. More recently, the author Suzanne Collins referenced the political power in controlling the price of bread in her sci-fi novels, *The Hunger Games*, set in a city called 'Panem'.

When the government in Egypt stopped subsidizing *aish*

baladi bread in 1977, because of the rising cost, there were riots. Dozens were killed and hundreds injured as the masses took to protesting on the streets, in what came to be known internationally as the 'Egyptian Bread Riots'. Thirty years later, in 2008, bread riots swept through the cities again. By this time, Egypt had become the most populous Arab nation, and a major importer of wheat. The country was exposed to fluctuations in global commodity prices. As wheat prices rose, bread shortages reached a critical point and became the focus of public anger. President Mubarak called in the army and police to bake bread, while he diverted foreign currency to buy more wheat on international markets. The same spike in global wheat prices precipitated bread riots in Bahrain, Yemen, Jordan and Morocco.

For Egyptians today, a ready supply of affordable bread is a basic human right, and something worth fighting for. During the 2011 uprising in Egypt, part of the Arab Spring, images of bread became central to the protest. In Tahrir Square, during the days of mass demonstrations, the cries were for *'aish, hurriya, karama insaniyya'* or 'bread, freedom and human dignity'. Of course, the pan-Arabic uprisings were about many things – state repression, corruption, representative government, citizenship and justice – but bread was, as so often in history, a common standard under which people rallied.

To limit popular uprisings, the price of bread was controlled throughout Europe, particularly during the late Middle Ages and the early modern era, when the majority of people drew the bulk of their calories from bread and scarcity was common. When harvests failed, or when flour supply chains collapsed because of war and people were deprived of bread, riots broke out like weeds in a field of young corn. The poor took to the streets in response to high prices during the Boston Bread Riot in 1713. There were riots about the price of flour in New York City in 1837, in southern Germany in 1847, and in the state of Virginia during the American Civil War, in 1863. More recently, demonstrators clamouring for bread marched through the streets of the Russian capital Petrograd, on 8 March 1917: a week later, four centuries of czarist rule ended when Nicholas II abdicated.

Perhaps the most famous bread riot of all took place on the eve of the French Revolution. This cataclysmic event in European history happened for many reasons, including a fiscal crisis, oppressive taxation and poor harvests due to the weather, but problems in supplying Paris with flour in the late eighteenth century meant that the spectre of hunger was ever present. On 5 October 1789, several thousand women marched out of Paris to Versailles, with crowbars, pitchforks and muskets, chanting 'Bread! Bread! Bread!' in the pouring rain. The next day, following the arrival of another mob at Versailles, the entire contents of the royal bread stores, including wagon-loads of grain and flour, trundled back to Paris. In the still pouring rain, the ranks of women chanted: 'Here comes the baker' and 'They're bringing the baker's wife' – the nicknames for Louis XVI and his consort Marie-Antoinette who, compelled by the mob, were also returning to the city.

The king and the queen were deposited at the Tuileries, where they remained under virtual house arrest until their execution, three years later. Marie-Antoinette almost certainly never uttered the famous line, 'Let them eat cake', in response to her subjects' demands for bread, yet the quote has stuck because it summarizes the privilege and hubris of a state that failed to provide even survival rations of bread to a starving peasantry.

'There were protests about bread again, recently,' Ahmed said as we re-joined the scrum on El Moez Street and drifted with the crowd into the gold market. 'We have subsidized bread today. It is only for families on the lowest income and you need a state-issued card to claim it, but there is a subsidized bakery in every neighbourhood in Cairo. Bread is still a sensitive subject. When we travel to Faqus tomorrow, if we are stopped by the police, you must not say you are researching a book about bread.'

Mohammed's field felt a world away from the maelstrom of the Old City. It was like being on an aural retreat after the cacophony of Cairo. Squatting next to Sa'id, I could hear the thump of the tractor engine driving the threshing machine, the muted cries of a football game on a dustbowl pitch beyond the graveyard, a barking dog and singing children. The sound-scape was overlaid with the constant, melodious music of the sickle at work in Mohammed's hand. The murmur of dried ears and awns brushing against each other as he gathered them was broken by the rasping sound of the scythe on the stalks.

Our shadows were lengthening across the bundles of wheat behind us now. The light was turning orange and thickening with dust. Mohammed waved a sickle over the wheat we had cut and explained the complex way the threshed grain is distributed. Ten per cent is apportioned as *Zakat*, a form of alms-giving and a religious obligation for Muslims. Another chunk is gifted to members of the wider family, then an amount goes to Mohammed's neighbours. The remainder is retained in the household, and while some is kept aside to make special breads for important religious events and family occasions, the greater part is simply used to make daily bread. I thought of my harvest. I wondered if I would have enough grain to be similarly munificent.

Walking back past the empty archaeologists' villa towards the car, Mohammed asked about my field. Was it sandy or did it hold water? Did it have to be aerated and weeded? How much seed had I planted? Did it all germinate? Had it tillered? Did the land need irrigating? I laughed: 'I live in Wales,' I said. 'Irrigation comes naturally from the sky.'

'It hasn't rained for a month. I'm not saying it's a disaster yet, but it's bad. And by the way, I had a quick look at your wheat. You've got powdery mildew,' Nick said. I bumped into him on the lane, mounted on his huge, snorting tractor like a maharajah on an elephant, looking sun-blasted and even more beleaguered than normal.

Powdery mildew is a distinctive fungal disease that affects many plants from soybeans and grapes to strawberries and melons. Along with ergot, loose smut, fusarium seedling blight, septoria, yellow rust, brown rust, stinking smut and various other bunts, powdery mildew is part of a large, unwelcome family of economically significant wheat diseases that, in a variety of ways, reduce yield. When I got to the field, you could not miss it. Many of the Hen Gymro plants had yellowing leaves covered in white pustules. It looked like half the plants were dying. The sight torpedoed my heart. I sent a photo to Ed Dickin, who replied straight away.

'Don't worry,' he said. 'Powdery mildew can only grow on living tissue, so the plants kill off their own leaves. The only action you can take to get rid of it is to spray with fungicide, and you're not going to do that. It won't cause significant yield loss, unless it gets into the upper leaves. Hopefully the plants will grow away from it.' They did. The ongoing dry weather certainly helped, but I wondered if my prayers in church, or perhaps my invocations of the winged harvest-goddess in the night sky, were being answered. Or maybe, just maybe, the wheat had responded to 'Baby, I Love You' by the Ramones. Either way, the Hen Gymro plants were over one metre tall and evidence of powdery mildew was receding by mid-June.

Almost magically, it happened. The field turned tawny, then gold. The plants became recognizable as wheat. The emmer heads were particularly exquisite. Each one comprised a ladder of seeds as long as a middle finger, stepped in a herringbone pattern with a flute of delicate awns. The heads soon began to bow over in a graceful arc, a physiological mechanism that protects the seeds from getting soaked by rain water on the stalk, which can cause them to sprout early. Not that they were likely to get wet. It hadn't rained properly in south-east Wales for weeks and the magazine *Farmers Weekly* was predicting the 'earliest wheat harvest in living memory'. In December, Ed Dickin had predicted my Hen Gymro would be ripe around the beginning of September, but the heatwave had torched that forecast. By the middle of July, harvest-time was imminent.

The optimal time to harvest depends on several factors

including the variety of wheat, the method of harvesting and whether the seed is to be milled into flour or saved and re-planted. When hand-cutting wheat for milling, it is best to harvest just before the grain is fully ripe, when it contains a larger proportion of starch and less bran. The drying process is completed either in the field, or under cover in a barn. Some growers and bakers believe slow-curing like this imparts a richer flavour to the flour, and thereby bread. When using a combine harvester, on the other hand, the grain must be com-pletely mature and dry: 'If you bite the grain and it breaks your teeth, it's ready,' Nick had said.

Each day I returned to the field. I took a seed head and rubbed it between my palms, as I had seen Mohammed do in the Nile Delta. At first, when I squeezed the grains between my thumb and forefinger, a milk-like liquid spilt out. A few days later, when the straw had turned golden-yellow, smooth and shiny and the chaff had a reddish-brown tint, the kernels oozed a thick, sticky, creamy dough when pinched. Still I waited. At the end of the third week in July, when I couldn't compress the kernels between my fingers any more, I bit one. The berry snapped. The wheat was ripe. It was time to reap.

For months, I had been nursing a romantic vision of what my field might look like at harvest-time. That vision was informed by landscape paintings depicting harvest scenes through the ages, which my wife had shown me: works by George Stubbs, John Linnell, George Mason, Van Gogh, Gauguin, Millet, Seurat, Constable (whose father was a flour miller) and others. One painting, in particular, stuck – *The Harvesters* by Pieter Bruegel the Elder. Painted in oil on wood in 1565, it was part of a series of six paintings that mark a watershed in the history of western art. For the first time, the religious pretext for landscape painting was replaced by humanism. Over time, all the images I'd seen began to merge in my mind's eye, into one epic harvest fantasy in which there were men in unbuttoned waistcoats at work with scythes and sickles, chest-deep in thick stands of wheat, goodly wives in broad-brimmed hats, laughing children, distant church spires, flagons of ale, victuals in wicker baskets being guarded by small boys, barking dogs, carts piled with straw and golden sheaves shining with nature's plenitude and grace.

The reality was different. On the day I decided to harvest, my family claimed they were busy, very busy. I had read that an honoured woman in the community, the 'grain mother', was traditionally called upon to cut the first sheaf, but my wife lampooned the suggestion: 'You can't rope me in that easily,' she said. I went to the field on my own, at dawn. If I wanted enough grain to make bread for a year, I would have to earn it with my own sweat. The earth was dry. Dust rose from my boots, as I ground them sideways to sink down on my haunches. The sickle rasped against the stalks and a handful of wheat plants came away in my hand. I cut what I could reach, rose and moved on. Each time I squatted, I cut an area the size of a bath. As the sun rose, casting orange talons across the earth, there were a dozen sheaves laid lengthwise behind me, waiting to be bundled with straw or string. The sky shifted from a pearlescent, arctic blue to cobalt and wisps of cloud drifted high over the hills. I thought of Mohammed. He would have been unimpressed with my wheat. The emmer was too thinly planted, or at least the winter flooding had made it sparse. The Hen Gymro was uneven in height and there were plenty of ears with little or no seed, called 'blind grain sites'.

Five dozen sheaves lay on the ground when my wife arrived with a basket of coffee, cider, sandwiches and bandages. I had already sliced into the back of my hand with the sickle, twice, and my forearm was painted with crimson streaks: 'Is this some kind of harvest snuff movie?' she said. Every time I stood up straight, unknown muscles in my lower back raged. We bundled the sheaves up and set them on end in sets, called 'stooks'. After lunch, the whole family piled into the field. My three children, bickering about what they should be paid, bundled more wheat. Then my neighbour arrived with her two young kids. On the promise of an ice cream, they all set about gleaning or gathering up the ears that had dropped from the stalks as we harvested.

In more straitened times, gleaning fields behind the harvest was a prerogative of the rural poor throughout Europe. It is a form of charity with biblical provenance. There are gleaners in Bruegel's painting. The practice was common into the twentieth century, but it inevitably petered out with the introduction of mechanical combine harvesters, which leave nothing but stubble. I did feel slightly like Dickens's character Fagin, with five children nipping ears off the ground between their nimble fingers, while I stood by swigging cider, but I needed every ear I could get. Then another neighbour, who happened to owe me half a day's labour, turned up carrying a machete. Finally, my field began to look faintly like a Flemish painting.

When we sat down for tea, cake and more cider, my wife took a handful of straw and tried to weave a simple corn dolly. Also known as 'kern-babbies' and 'mell dolls' in Britain, corn dollies are part of a tradition that stretches back to ancient times. At the end of the wheat harvest under the pharaohs, stalks from the last sheaf were plaited into fans or hollow shapes in which the corn-goddess or spirit could take refuge until the following growing season, when the dolly was ploughed back into the earth, in the first furrow. This goddess of fertility, the 'Harvest Mother' or 'Corn Maiden', has been imagined anew by almost every crop-growing society since. Corn dollies were commonly hung in farmhouses and barns, as a symbol of our profound and enduring relationship with the land and its progeny. The ritual of making corn dollies in Britain gently died out in the 1950s, and my wife's effort – a crude representation of a floppy maiden coming apart at the sides – was unlikely to revive it. But, in recognition of the truth that we all need to be more attuned to the endowment of the earth, I placed the corn dolly in the back of the car, to be hung in the threshing barn at home.

As the setting sun clipped the purple-headed mountains, we gathered the picnic detritus and the tools together. There was still wheat to be cut. I would be back in the field tomorrow, taking more lumps out of my hand. The car and the trailer were already overbrimming with the earth's bounty, though. We were all tired, sun-baked and ready for a swim in the river.

CHAPTER 3

Every Corn Its Own Chaff:
Threshing and Winnowing

'Eat the bread now, O Enkidu, as it belongs to life'
– *The Epic of Gilgamesh*

After the pleasure of being in the field watching the wheat grow, followed by the antediluvian satisfaction of gathering the harvest, the chore of separating the edible grains of wheat from the indigestible husks was a significant comedown. Threshing by hand is laborious, stultifying, dirty, inefficient, primitive work. No one tells you this. It is like having your first child – you get a lot of advice and encouragement about pregnancy and birth, but no one says you'll be punching yourself in the face with a mixture of exhaustion and boredom before the baby is a month old.

Until the mechanization of farming in the nineteenth century, threshing was, as with many tedious but essential farm tasks, a communal activity. Large families or wider networks of people gathered to socialize while separating the wheat from the chaff. I put it to my family: 'I'm having a threshing bee. We're going to party like Gatsby – all over the wheat,' I said. They were intrigued. 'Bee', as in 'sewing bee', is an old Anglo-American term for a mutual work gathering. I opened up the barn at home. It would have been a threshing barn once, with two large double doors aligned to the prevailing wind in the valley. While threshing was always an outdoor activity on sun-baked mud floors beside the Mediterranean, the Greek geographer and explorer Pytheas, who visited Britain in 325 BC, noted how northern Europeans threshed undercover in great barns, to keep the grain dry. I pegged a tarpaulin sheet to the floor and covered it with Hen Gymro wheat. I rigged a speaker up and compiled a foot-stomping playlist. My girls invited their friends over. I even made a jug of punch. It started with a pop. We all ground the soles of our shoes and boots into the golden ears on the floor, to the sweet riffs of 'Harvest For the World' by the Isley Brothers. Then the girls were gone, back into the house, to post the briefest threshing bee ever on Instagram. I was left dancing alone, watched by the cat.

I tried a flail next. The flail is an ancient implement with roots in all cereal-growing cultures. It comprises two pieces of wood joined by a section of rope, leather or chain. Once commonplace, the flail is best known today in its revised form as a popular martial arts weapon, the nunchaku. With a flail, the user wields the longer piece of wood; the shorter piece swings through the air on the flexible hinge and thrashes into the wheat, dislodging the grains from their casings. Simon, a neighbour and friend from our community woodland group,

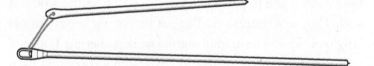

offered to make me a flail. Simon is a criminal barrister by day
and a wood-turner by night. We met outside the post office
in my local market town for the hand over. He had made three
flails.

'I've been getting some funny looks, walking through
town with a collection of martial arts weaponry. The first
two are prototypes. It's time to release your inner Bruce Lee,'
he said.

In the barn, I arranged a sheaf of Hen Gymro inside a sack.
Prototype I – a broom handle attached to a flat metal bar by
a chain – lasted two strikes. With the third swing of the handle, the metal bar came free, catapulting the length of the
building into a stone wall – more 'Enter the Dragon' than I
was hoping for. Eyeing me warily, my dogs backed outside.
prototype II lasted a few minutes longer, but prototype III –
two poles of coppiced ash attached with a leather hinge – was
effective.

At first, flailing was invigorating. There was a degree of
ergonomic pleasure in whirling the 'swinging stick', as it was
once called, and a satisfying thwack when it landed on target.
After ten minutes, I developed a feeling for it. After twenty
minutes, I was bored. Shortly after that, it began to feel like
penal work. I couldn't be sure if this was the nature of the
task itself, or a measure of how time has accelerated since the
era when the flail was omnipresent. I thought of Benjamin
Franklin, the American statesman and polymath. During the
American War of Independence, he designed a paper currency.
His two-dollar bill shows a flail over sheaves of wheat with
the motto 'Tribulatio Ditat' or 'It is enriched by affliction'.

Republican propaganda, of course, but at least my tribulations were not new.

I pulled the wheat stalks out of the sack and checked the ears. Many of the small, reddish grains had separated. They were in a pile at the bottom under a drift of flaxen chaff. Some were still firmly attached to their stalks, though, sealed inside their coats of plant material called lemmas and paleas. Succumbing to my deepest OCD tendencies and ignoring for now the basic economic law of diminishing marginal returns, I rubbed and pinched every last grain free in my fingers. Then I picked out the rogue oats and grit. When I had threshed two sheaves, I inspected the pile of grain. There was enough to make a bread roll. And the afternoon was gone. This was going to take weeks.

To speed the process up, I drove a car back and forth over some wheat. I saw this method on a cobbled lane near Lake Ohrid in Albania, years ago. A farmer there had scattered his wheat across the road and left passing motorists and the wind to undertake the work. This is the modern take on driving oxen or donkeys around in circles, pulling a heavy board or sleigh over sheaves scattered on a hard, smooth floor – a method likely devised by the Phoenicians in ancient times and represented in Egyptian tomb paintings dating from the Old Kingdom. My car tyres worked little better than the flail, though. With growing impatience, I took a bootload of wheat to a friend's organic smallholding and spent a day using his foot-powered thresher, a device popular among small-scale rice producers in Asia. There was an Amish asceticism to this, particularly after the bellicose nature of flailing, but it was still noisy, dusty and again, slow. I was, at last, nearing the end of my Hen Gymro. Back at home, I finished it off, banging handfuls of stalks against the inside of a galvanized steel dustbin. I was weary of threshing, and I hadn't even begun with the emmer. I wanted help. I know what Lenin said – 'He who does not work, neither shall he eat' – but I didn't care any more. I wanted a machine.

The first successful threshing machine was designed and built in 1786 by Andrew Meikle, a son of the Scottish Enlightenment. Remarkably, it was the first major advance in the wheat harvesting and production process since the time of the pharaohs. Meikle was a millwright and mechanical engineer from East Lothian, near Edinburgh. His 'portable' machine, an evolution as all great mechanical 'inventions' inevitably are, used fluted rollers to feed sheaves of cereals into a rotating drum that beat the ears against a curved casing at high speed – basically what I was doing inside the steel dustbin, just a lot faster and without the tea breaks. The seeds and the chaff then fell through sieves, while the straw was extracted. The drum could be driven by water, horses or other forms of power. At the time, it was a sophisticated machine using gears to feed cereals into the rollers at an optimum rate. Having added a fan that effectively winnowed the grain from the chaff, Meikle began production in 1789. By 1800, threshing machines were popular across Lowland Scotland and spreading fast into England. The age of the flail, an immemorial agricultural tool that would have been, for millennia, as common as smart phones are today, was finally ending.

Not everyone welcomed the untiring jaws of Meikle's machine, though. For the armies of landless agricultural workers in England at this time, the newfangled contraption took away their livelihoods. In winter, when there were few paid jobs on farms, freelance labourers relied on threshing work. It has been estimated that threshing used one quarter of all agricultural manpower in Europe. The machines stirred a wave of discontent that came to a head in south-east England in 1830, with a popular uprising called the 'Swing Riots'. There were outbreaks of arson and riot for several months, as gangs of labourers roved through all the major grain-growing counties chanting 'Bread or blood', burning properties and smashing the principal object of their ire – threshing machines. Threatening letters signed 'Captain Swing' were sent to landowners, magistrates and parsons. 'Swing' likely refers to the 'swinging stick' or flail, which the labourers had formerly wielded to earn their winter-coin.

The Swing Riots were heavily suppressed by the government. They were part of a wider, early nineteenth-century trend of social and political unrest triggered by rural depression and chronic underemployment among landless labourers, not just in Britain, but across northern France and Belgium too. On the other side of the Atlantic Ocean, however, where there was abundant land and a shortage of people, no one was smashing threshing machines. Quite the reverse – they could not make them fast enough.

As farmers spread into the American Midwest during the first half of the nineteenth century, a corps of blacksmiths and mechanics with few formal engineering skills but pails of

enterprise set out to make farming less labour-intensive. Threshing machines, mowing machines, John Deere's self-polishing,
cast-steel plough (patented in 1837) and, critically, reaping
machines were put to great effect in transforming agriculture in
general, and the cultivation of cereals in particular. Many American farms at this time were ploughed and harrowed with horses.
Cereal crops, however, were still generally sown, harvested,
threshed and winnowed by hand, just as they had been in ancient
Egypt. Harvesting by hand was a particular problem, because
of the high stakes. While farmers can roughly choose when to
plough, sow, weed, thresh and winnow, the harvest must be
gathered on time, when the cereals are ripe, otherwise all is
lost – 'soon ripe, soon rotten', as the proverb goes. Inevitably,
there was a shortage of labour at harvest-time, just as there had
been along the Nile, 6,000 years earlier. The issue was exacerbated in America, though, by bigger farms and fewer people.

There were many rivals in the race to mechanize harvesting
and threshing – as Victor Hugo once remarked, 'You can
resist an invading army; you cannot resist an idea whose time
has come.' A Scottish clergyman named Patrick Bell, John
Ridley in Australia and Obed Hussey in the USA, among
others, invented reaping machines around this time, while,
in 1835, Hiram Moore patented a machine that both cut and
threshed wheat. However, one name became synonymous
with popularizing the horse-drawn reaping machine, that of
a man who would eventually be ennobled with the title 'the
Father of Modern Agriculture' – Cyrus Hall McCormick.

Born in 1809 on a farm near Lexington, in the Blue Ridge
Mountains of Virginia, McCormick was the eldest of eight

children in a well-to-do family of hardy, Scots-Irish heritage.
With a keen understanding of mechanics and a handful of
minor agricultural inventions already to his name, McCormick
began to manufacture horse-drawn reapers on a small scale
in the 1830s. Sales were slow. In 1847, he moved west – like
the new wave of European immigrants, following the sun
away from the Old World – to set up a factory in the freshly
minted metropolis of Chicago. His timing was perfect. The
following year, Chicago, a marshy fur trappers' village in 1815
and the 'city of the Plains' by mid-century, got its first canal,
railroad, telegraph, stockyard, grain elevator (a tall building
used to store seed) and Board of Trade. McCormick marketed
his machines, which could now do the work of five men and
harvest ten acres a day, across the Midwest. There, prairie
farmers were producing a growing share of the nation's wheat
on larger, uniform farms, and looking for a solution to high
labour costs and manpower shortages at harvest season.

McCormick had several qualities that set him apart: he
tinkered endlessly with his invention; he was a tenacious busi-
nessman who pioneered agency contracts, instalment-selling
and written warranties; he marketed and exhibited tirelessly (in
1851, McCormick brought his reaping machine to the Great
Exhibition at Crystal Palace in London, where it won a gold
medal and attracted international buyers); finally, he was a zeal-
ous Presbyterian on a God-given mission to feed the world. In
1854, when the railroads west of Chicago reached and then
crossed the Mississippi River, sales took off. In 1856, the McCormick Harvesting Machine Company sold 4,000 reapers. By the
outbreak of the American Civil War, in 1861, there were tens

of thousands of reapers at work on American farms. Edwin Masters, Secretary of War under President Lincoln, noted at the time: 'The reaper is for the North what the slave is for the South. It releases our young men to do battle for the Union, and at the same time, keeps up the supply of the nation's bread.'

The success of McCormick's reaper heralded a new era of agricultural prosperity for America. The production of wheat increased significantly during the 1850s and then again, to the consternation of many, during the 1860s, even as the Civil War raged. According to Senator William H. Seward, in 1860, 'owing to Mr McCormick's invention, the line of civilization moves westward thirty miles each year'. Just as Lincoln was calling every third man to join the Union army, wheat production swelled by 50 per cent or more in Ohio, Illinois, Indiana, Iowa and Wisconsin, principally because of machinery. Wheat provided bread and bread meant victory. No one in the North went hungry, while soldiers were given the best bread. In the South, they could not eat cotton.

In the seventeenth century, wheat had been of no importance to the Pilgrim Fathers and their scions. They couldn't get it to grow. They had survived on bread made from rye and maize, called 'rye and injun'. In the 1770s, George Washington experimented with different varieties of wheat at Mount Vernon. Still, few farmers bothered to grow it as the nineteenth century dawned. By 1876, however, just twelve years after the Civil War and only thirty years after McCormick opened his manufacturing plant in Chicago, America became the world's largest producer of wheat.

There was even surplus grain to export, from Chicago to

Europe. In the Old World, a metamorphosis in taste during the early nineteenth century, largely inspired by the French, meant the majority of European people now wanted bread made from wheat, rather than the common grains of the Middle Ages and the early modern period, rye and barley. In Britain, the Corn Laws, which had imposed heavy tariffs on imported cereals including wheat for forty years, were finally repealed in 1846, following the horrors of the Irish Potato Famine and pressure exerted by the Anti-Corn Law League. It was a major victory for free trade over protectionism, providing cheap bread to fire the industrialization of Britain. Similar tariffs were removed in Germany in 1865. The Crimean War, a succession of poor harvests in the 1870s and the Great Agricultural Depression in Britain during the last decades of the century offered further incentive for America to channel her river of wheat towards Europe. With the outbreak of the First World War, wheat imports from the USA, and by this time Canada too, became critical. Neither Germany nor Russia had mechanized agriculture by this time. Canada shipped wheat to her friends, including Britain, France, Belgium and Greece, throughout the war. In the perilous spring of 1917, American President Woodrow Wilson nationalized foreign trade in grain. The moment America took sides, the moment the Great Plains became the bread basket of the Allies, the equipoise of the Great War shifted.

Farm mechanization continued apace through the beginning of the twentieth century. The railroads reached further into the Great Plains, the vast expanse of flat grassland and steppe west of the Mississippi River and east of the Rocky Mountains, extending almost the length of the USA and far into Canada, where fertile lands well suited to growing wheat and new farming methods were ready for the plough. Some 400 million acres, more than ten times the size of England and Wales, were brought under cultivation in North America during the period 1860–1900. It had now replaced Britain as the centre of developments in agricultural technology. There were new mechanical mowers, crushers, corn-cutters, potato planters, hay driers and windrowers. In 1872, the Deering Company in Chicago built the first successful reaper-binder, a machine that not only cut wheat, but successfully tied it into bundles too. Threshing machines were still stationary, and powered by traction engines, but it was inevitable that the three separate operations – reaping, threshing and winnowing – would soon be undertaken by a single machine. By the 1880s, 'reaper-threshers' were being trialled in many parts of the USA, pulled by teams of up to forty horses or mules. Around the turn of the twentieth century, steam power was introduced. By the 1920s, the first tractor-pulled reaper-threshers with combustion engines were in the fields. The age of the horse was ending.

In 1938, the world's first successful self-propelled harvesting machine – the Massey Harris Model 20 – called a 'combine harvester' for the first time, went on the market. It was another small step in harvesting technology (the threshing part of the Massey Harris process was similar in principle to Meikle's original design), but a great bound forward in humankind's efforts to master its environment. A revolution in manpower, arguably the greatest upheaval in agriculture since the advent of farming, had taken place. In a few decades, machines had transformed the wheat industry in North America, with lasting impact on pastoral society, the global economy and our diet.

The mechanization of wheat production also marked the birth of a dystopian age for nature, not just in the American Midwest, but in agriculturally rich lands around the globe. The epic, annual drudgery of threshing by hand was finally over, and the hiss of a flail landing on a sheaf of wheat was reduced to a feeble folk memory. With its passing, the collectivist traditions and ideals of the European peasants who first broke the sod on the Great Plains died too. A new epoch in the long history of cereals, and in the story of bread, had begun.

'When I ordered my first new combine in 1974, it cost me $27,000. I was so proud. And this combine here, well, it cost me about $500,000. And I got six of 'em,' Jim Diebert said, lifting his baseball cap and waving it at the gleaming green machine behind him. We were in a field in South Dakota. In one direction, where the land rippled away from us like a mid-ocean swell, all I could see was wheat. In another direction, fields ran down into a golden basin with ribs of green and brown where dirt roads led to farmsteads hidden by clumps of trees, all beneath a blue sky. In the far distance, rain was falling in angled, grey drainpipes from a thunderhead cloud. Half a kilometre away, I could see Jim's other five combines, slicing through a wheat field with drifts of shredded chaff rising behind them like gun smoke from ships of the line in an eighteenth-century naval battle.

Jim has been 'custom harvesting' or 'custom combining' – cutting crops for different farmers across the Great Plains, as part of an itinerant crew – for nearly five decades. He is now head of the Association of U.S. Custom Harvesters. Short, broad and stout like a rugby prop forward, with forearms the size of fire extinguishers, Jim was difficult to age. I had guessed fifty-five years old. Then I asked – sixty-seven. He wore the uniform of the American Outback: a branded mesh baseball cap, short-sleeved work shirt, leather belt with a large buckle, pliers in a holster, blue jeans and brown, heeled boots.

When I contacted Jim in late July, to see if I could join his operation for a few days, I was 1,800km away in Texas. He said: 'Sure. Come up Route 83 to Quinn, South Dakota. Turn north at the "Two-bit Steak House". You'll see our camp beside the road. Locals call it "Diebert-ville".' The directions seemed a little thin, to locate a transient campsite in a country of 9.8 million square kilometres, but I found him first time.

US Route 83 runs north–south, from Canada to Mexico, for 3,034km, bisecting the 'Wheat Belt'. It ought to be a fabled highway, yet few of my American friends could even place it on a map. I wondered if this was because American history, with the notable exception of the Civil War, is configured on the east–west axis: the pioneers, the wagon trains, the Lewis and Clark Expedition across the Continental Divide, the Gold Rush, Brigham Young's Mormon Exodus, trans-continental railroads, Route 66 and the Lincoln Highway have together burnt the east–west axis into the national consciousness.

'Nope,' Jim said. 'Nobody's heard of Route 83 because this is "Flyover Country".' The pejorative term derives from the fact that most Americans only ever see these heartland states from the air, flying back and forth between the metropolitan agglomerations on the east and west coasts. I drove north on 83 for two days. I crossed railroad tracks and interstate high- ways, all on the other axis. I tuned the radio to religious music channels and listened to long guitar ballads about sin. I passed road signs that said: 'Don't die, drive safely', 'Correctional facility: do not stop for hitch hikers' and 'Wear fur'. I photo- graphed implausibly delicate bands of violet-tinted clouds pressed into gunmetal-grey skies. I watched numerous grain elevators, known as 'Kansas skyscrapers', rise from silver horizons like cathedral spires out of the East Anglian fens or giant windmills from the plains of La Mancha.

All the towns looked the same. In between them, the fields and farms were square. The whole geography of the Great Plains was alien to me. Everything is projected on a ruled grid. I stopped often, either beside the highway or a short distance down a dirt track. I sat on the roof of the car and felt like a surfer sitting on a beach, searching the sea for swell. Every matchbox of land in this vast, flat industrial 'agri-scape' is cul- tivated, at the expense of nature. There were no insects and birds in the air, and no worms in the soil when I turned clumps of earth over. The varied grassland ecosystems that existed when the first European immigrants arrived were habitats for dozens of species of migratory songbirds, mammals and native butterflies; that diversity was sacrificed to make space for crop- land, and a golden torrent of grain. Nature has been quelled, sprayed, stripped, shaven, drilled and repressed by the unflag- ging righteousness of man. I tried to imagine what these prairies might have looked like when the first settlers, or 'sod- busters' as they were known, arrived and ploughed it up to plant wheat. I tried to imagine how those German, Norwegian and Ukrainian families must have felt, wheeling their carts into a million square kilometres of grassland where elk and buffalo roamed. If they were overawed, it was momentary.

The first farmers settled in the Great Plains on 160-acre plots of land called 'quarter sections', given away for free under the Homestead Act of 1862, signed by Abraham Lincoln. Life was raw, but the soil, following the accumulation of organic matter over millennia, was excellent. Once the homesteaders had torn out the rich root systems of the perennial prairie grasses and planted seeds, healthy crops rose up, particularly wheat. Initially, the settlers grew wheat to make bread at home, as their impoverished ancestors had done in Europe, to survive. Their bread was the story of who they were. Within three decades, though, their annual harvest was integral to the emerging industrial economy of the USA. Wheat had become a commodity.

In the 1850s, the Chicago Board of Trade, a private organization set up by grain traders, introduced a system to categorize wheat that set standards for quality. Generally, the plumpest, purest, cleanest, driest and heaviest grain made the top grade, securing the best price. Did it also make the healthiest bread? Did it even make the tastiest bread? No one asked. More importantly, the new system severed the link between a physical product of human labour and ownership rights. Traders now bought and sold 'elevator receipts' – abstract claims on the stream of grain that flowed through Chicago – rather than an actual sack of wheat with a farmer's mark on it.

These elevator receipts became a new form of money,

secured by grain. Soon, the receipts themselves were traded on the floor of the Chicago Exchange, while the price of wheat travelled back and forth to New York on the new telegraph wires. The market for grain (and the price of bread) now had less to do with the soils and climate of Kansas and Oklahoma, and more to do with European wars and the flow of information about the economy in general.

Trading cereals was nothing new, of course. Financiers have been buying and selling wheat since farmers first created a surplus in the Fertile Crescent. The Athenian orator and speech writer Lysias railed against the rapacity of grain dealers in 386 BC, at the end of the Corinthian War. What happened next in Chicago, though, was entirely novel. For the first time, speculators began gambling on future movements in the price of wheat in an organized fashion, at scale. The market was no longer in the grain itself. The market was now in the *price* of grain.

It is difficult to say exactly when the 'futures market' in wheat began, but it was certainly established when the Homestead Act was passed. By 1875, the financial trade in grain futures was worth ten times Chicago's actual grain business. This transformation of wheat from a foodstuff that many farmers still effectively produced by hand to an abstruse symbol of capitalism – something you 'shorted' rather than harvested, or 'cornered' rather than winnowed – had consequences for society across the world. It was the first significant move in a process that would eventually divorce bread from agriculture completely. It was the beginning of the 'financialization' of our food system.

By the start of the twentieth century, the farmers of the

Great Plains were already becoming disillusioned. Many had been lured by the money men in Chicago into trying to grow enough wheat for two continents, just as the initial period of intense soil fertility ended and yields began to decline. Perhaps because of the seemingly inexhaustible fund of fecund land, or perhaps because of the commoditization of the produce, agriculture on the Great Plains tied itself up in the culture of extraction at all costs. European soil management practices, like crop rotation involving clover and turnips, were discarded early on, as the ecologically distinct and diverse grasslands were replaced with vast monocultures worked by machines. Meanwhile, the dream of free men on free soil was crucified in the banality of unpaid mortgages: 'In God we trusted, in Kansas we busted', the adage went.

Farming was already a far cry from the homesteaders' original paradigm of redoubtable, self-sufficient families on small plots when, in the early 1930s, the rain abruptly stopped. A consequence of farming practices, and in a terrifying exemplum of man's hubris, the last of the rich soil on the Great Plains then turned to dust and, in high winds, literally blew away in 'black blizzards'. This period of drought and severe storms, which came to be known as the 'Dust Bowl', lasted the decade. By 1940, the area of agricultural destitution stretched from Nebraska to northern Texas, via Oklahoma and Kansas. Crops, notably wheat, failed again and again, and tens of thousands of impoverished farmers abandoned their family properties and migrated west.

Custom harvesting, Jim explained, began during the Second World War, when a shortage of both labour and machinery, exacerbated by the wartime intensification of food production, precipitated the next crisis on the Great Plains. By necessity, gangs of men set off with whatever machinery they could muster to harvest for every farmer without the means. In peacetime, the practice continued. It released small farmers from heavy capital investment in combines, while it made maximum use out of these high-value machines.

The practice of hiring gangs or 'brigades' of itinerant labourers to cut wheat is almost as old as harvesting itself, though it probably reached a peak around the beginning of the twentieth century, shortly before the introduction of the combine. Then, there were mass migrations of men with their scythes and sickles at harvest-time, from Ireland to England, Spain to France, Austria to Germany and Italy to Argentina. In 1903, 28,000 itinerant men were recruited as reapers in Kansas alone.

Jim lives in Colby, Kansas. He leaves home in the second week of May each year, at the head of a 3km-long convoy comprising six combines, grain carts, service trucks, lorries and mobile homes for his seasonal crew of fresh-faced wheat gypsies from around the world. This harvest, the fifteen young lads were from France, Zimbabwe, Australia, Britain and the USA.

The crew initially head south on the 'harvest trail' to Texas. Then they turn north, effectively following the wheat as it ripens (at roughly 30km a day), stopping to harvest in Oklahoma (early June), Kansas (late June), South Dakota (July) and North Dakota (August), before returning home. It is a 3,500km round trip, to harvest 40,000 acres of wheat for fifty different farmers. If the weather is right, they harvest six days a week. On Sundays, they go to church.

'We get home in early September. It's a nomadic way of life. We're like a travelling circus. And I guess I'm the head clown,' Jim said, hauling himself up a ladder and into the cab. 'Come on up. Time we cut some wheat.'

As the combine rolled forward, the sharp triangular cutters within the wide 'header' – the maws of the monster – sucked a swathe of glinting wheat through the turning rakes and into the belly of the machine. The threshing mechanism separated the grain while a jet of air blew the chaff away. The grain spewed into the hopper. The straw was hustled to the back of the combine, chopped and spat back on to the field in a jet. I wondered what Meikle and McCormick would make of this mindboggling machine that can cut, thresh, winnow and clean 200 acres of wheat a day. Behind my head, I could see the grain pouring into the hopper like liquid caramel. Jim jabbed one of the two touchscreen displays in front of him with a finger: 'Says we've cut 1,000lb of wheat since we started.' Around 500kg, enough for 850 loaves of bread, I thought, and we'd been cutting for only minutes.

Despite the technology in the combine, which includes GPS, digital cameras on the grain and tailings elevators, computer software that monitors harvesting performance and sensors that relay moisture readings, Jim still walks in the fields, inspects the wheat stalks and even bites the grains, just as Mohammed does in the Nile Delta, to know precisely when to harvest: 'My dentist told me to quit chewing wheat, but all that old-fashioned stuff, it's just what you do,' he said.

When the hopper in the combine was full, the computer alerted Jim and he radioed the grain-cart driver. From the cart, the grain was transferred to a lorry at the field edge and ferried back to the farm, to be stored in a huge metal silo, Jim explained. From there, it is hauled to an elevator, at the local railroad terminal. There it is weighed and tested for protein strength, before being loaded on to freight trains. Standard 'unit' trains comprise 110 cars, are up to 2km long, and carry 400,000 bushels (10,000 tonnes). The trains trundle south to Galveston on the Gulf of Mexico or west to Portland, Oregon. From there, the grain is transported to industrial millers or shipped around the world.

'Right now, our country can't sell wheat anywhere. The world wheat market has gone to hell,' Jim said. 'The last two years – '16 and '17 – have been the toughest two years of my harvesting career. The farmers are going away from the wheat, trying to find something else to grow to make a profit. Take this farm, it went from 20,000 acres of wheat to 12,000 in one year. Wheat'll be here a hundred years after I'm gone – bread is just a staple of life – but these are rough years.'

As Jim swung the combine round to cut another swathe, he told me the farm was on the climatic border between the domains of winter wheat and spring wheat. South of here, all the way to Texas, winter wheat is preferred. To the north, through the Dakotas and into the Canadian prairies, spring wheat is grown. The vast plethora of wheat varieties is further divided in North America into four main classes – hard red, hard white, soft red and soft white. 'Red' refers to the colour of the grain that varies from white to dark red, according to the amount of pigment in the outer coat or 'pericarp' of the seed. 'Hard' refers to the texture of the kernels that varies from steely and vitreous to soft and starchy. Importantly, hard wheat has a high protein content, which generally means the flour is good for baking leavened breads. Soft wheat has less protein and a higher percentage of carbohydrates; the flour is more suitable for making cakes, pastries, cookies, crackers, doughnuts, breakfast cereals and more. Prior to the introduction of hard wheats in the late nineteenth century, bread in America and Canada was made from soft white wheat flour, and frequently mixed with rye, barley or oats. Generally, it was baked at home. The bread was probably flavoursome, but it would have been dense. Most of the grain planted today between Texas and South Dakota is hard red winter wheat. Heading north, it is mostly hard red spring wheat.

Being in the cab of Jim's combine was like being on his front porch. We chatted away about religion, industrial injuries ('I got a leg chewed in a corn header once, but I can still walk,' he said), the impact of automation ('Combines that drive themselves are not far away'), tornadoes, Trump (Jim was a fan), trade wars with China, fighting for farmers in 'DC' and rural depopulation. I had read that the number of farms, and the number of people on farms, in the USA halved in the period 1950–75; the trend was most apparent in the Wheat Belt and related to mechanization. Today, another wave of farm consolidation is sending the rural population into demographic freefall again. The Wheat Belt is emptying out, even as the rest of the country grows more densely populated.

For long periods, we fell silent, as you might on an ocean voyage. Being a man of the Great Plains, Jim was comfortable with silence. Occasionally, he broke the tranquillity with a pair of pliers. 'The farmers I cut wheat for are friends, and friends are riches. Everybody I know has got money is miserable. I'd do this all again. I enjoy it. When it comes time to go to harvest next year, I'll be ready. Hell, I'll probably die in a wheat field somewhere.'

It is hard to believe, but wheat did not thrive on the Great Plains at first. That changed when a colony of 18,000 immigrants belonging to the peace-loving Mennonite Christian sect arrived in Kansas from Ukraine, in 1874. Being cereal farmers, the Mennonites carried with them trunks full of a wheat variety called 'Turkey Red', a diverse landrace population from the fields between the Dnieper River and the Sea of Azov, on the Black Sea. The climate of southern Ukraine – hot summers, occasional droughts and cold winters – proved to be remarkably similar to Kansas. Turkey Red yielded well in its new home. It was the first hard red winter wheat to be grown in America and it quickly became the primary wheat of the Great Plains. By 1900, Turkey Red was planted on five million acres in Kansas alone. By 1919, it made up 99 per cent of the entire winter wheat crop in the USA, helping to establish the American Wheat Belt as the bread basket of the world in the early twentieth century.

As Turkey Red was transforming the agricultural economy of the USA, another variety of wheat was having a similar effect further north. In 1842, David Fife, a Scottish immigrant farmer in Ontario, received a packet of wheat seeds from a friend back home – a fortuitous event that changed the destiny of Canada. Ed Dickin had told me that the packet of seeds originated in Ukraine, like Turkey Red, though it was probably from the region of Galicia, 1,000km north-west of the Sea of Azov. Fife's handful of grain was different from Turkey Red in one fundamental way – it was the first hard *spring* wheat to be planted on the American continent. Red Fife, as the variety came to be known, suited the soils of Manitoba, Saskatchewan and Alberta. It yielded well and produced high-quality baking flour. Between 1860 and 1900, Red Fife became the dominant wheat variety in the Prairie Provinces of Canada and the northernmost states of the USA. There was, however, one significant problem with Red Fife. It matured late in the year and, in Canada at least, yields were often affected by early autumnal frosts. To rectify this, and to expand wheat's range even further north, Canadian farmers needed a variety of wheat that matured before the frosts.

The scientific discipline of plant breeding was still in its infancy at this time. Gregor Mendel, a monk and amateur botanist known today as the 'father of genetics', discovered the basic principles of heredity in the mid-nineteenth century, by hybridizing pea plants in the garden of his monastery in Brno, in what is now the Czech Republic. His priceless contribution to science, which laid the foundations for a new abundance of wheaten bread around the planet, was forgotten for forty years, however. Around 1906, the Swedish geneticist Herman Nilsson-Ehle confirmed Mendel's law in his work with wheat plants. By demonstrating that economically important characteristics in wheat are inherited, and may be recombined in a specific way, Nilsson-Ehle opened up the practical application of genetics to plant breeding. Botany (with a bit of help from mathematics and the laws of heredity) now had the upper hand on climate.

Dr Charles Saunders, a Canadian chemist and wheat breeder, set about trying to fix the 'fault' in Red Fife by crossing it with other varieties. Despite Nilsson-Ehle's work, this was still a radical idea. In 1907, Saunders successfully crossed Red Fife with a variety from India, called Hard Red Calcutta. The result was a cultivar called Marquis, one of the most successful varieties of wheat the world has ever known. It was launched commercially in 1909. Winter-hardy, early-maturing, shorter in height and high-yielding, Marquis quickly became the cornerstone of wheat production in western Canada. The milling and baking qualities attracted universal renown. The wheat fields of the Prairie Provinces expanded from under seven million acres in 1901 to seventeen million acres, 90 per cent of which was planted with Marquis, in just twenty years. By 1940, Canada had become one of the greatest wheat-exporting nations in the world, dubbed 'the Granary of the British Empire'.

From the beginning of agriculture in the Fertile Crescent, wheat – and to a great extent bread culture – had been confined by climate to moist, maritime areas in the intermediate latitudes or temperate zones of the planet. Too far north, wheat froze in the ground; nearer the equator, it burnt on the stalk. From the 1860s, a redistribution of the crop's geographical variants, followed by advances in wheat breeding, changed this. Cultivation expanded and shifted into drier continental zones with shorter growing seasons – the Great Plains, Central Asia, Siberia – and also into drier, warmer climes like Australia,

Argentina and South Africa. These new bread baskets were land rich but people poor. Agriculture was only possible because of mechanization and the railways. In little more than a generation, agronomists, botanists and, in time, chemists completely re-drew the wheat map of the world. Arguably, only just in time.

In 1798, Thomas Robert Malthus had famously forecast a population crash based on his calculation that it was impossible to increase wheat yields as fast as people procreated. Between 1850 and 1900, the population of Europe and North America expanded fast, from 300 to 500 million, prompting renewed, *fin de siècle* anxiety that a 'Malthusian catastrophe' involving mass famine and disease was imminent. The mechanization of farming, the spread of wheat cultivation and the new league of plant breeders, or the 'hunger fighters' as they were later known, like Saunders in Canada, William Farrer in Australia and Mark Carleton in the USA, together removed the threat of starvation in developed countries. Today, largely as a result of their work, wheat is reaped and threshed somewhere in the world every month of the year: in Australia and Argentina the harvest happens in January; India, Brazil and Uruguay in February and March; Iran, North Africa and Mexico in April; in May, wheat ripens in China, southern Spain and Texas; Italy and California in June; Ukraine and Canada in July; England, Germany and Scandinavia in August; Scotland in September; large parts of Russia in October; South Africa and Peru in November; and Ethiopia in December.

Saunders, with his chemistry doctorate, probably grasped the relationship between protein content in wheat and the volume of a loaf better than most. He understood that wheat with high protein content (12–16 per cent by weight, in the case of hard spring wheats) yields flour that makes dough which absorbs more water and expands further, to produce bread with better structure and greater volume. Saunders not only chewed seeds to get a sense of their protein content, he also milled them and baked bread, noting the texture, shape, colour and volume of his loaves. He was not just looking for a new variety of wheat that could survive in the Alberta Badlands, he was also searching for an expedient wheat that met with the radical technological advances then taking place in the milling industry, and one which could survive the intensity of mixing machines in industrial bakeries, to produce a new style of bread for the modern world.

After the interminable toil of threshing, the joy of winnowing, the final part of the process to separate the grain from the chaff, came as a surprise. I loved almost everything about it. I loved how I got better at it quickly. I loved the way you started each round of winnowing with a mound of chaff and seed. With every toss, a heap of plant material departed and the grain emerged in the basket like a 'magic eye' illusion or stereogram.

With the delicacy reserved for a drop shot in tennis, I lifted the flat basket or 'winnowing fan' up and down in one movement. The contents rose lazily into the air. A hundred flecks of yellow chaff momentarily formed an evanescent sculpture, before swirling like a murmuration of miniature starlings, and scattering on the ground under a lime tree. The wheat berries pattered back into the basket. I shook the basket from side to side, to order the contents in the right ovoid formation, stooped slightly and tossed again. I thought of Patrick Kavanagh, one of my favourite poets: 'Ordinary things wear lovely wings,' he wrote.

I became attuned to the minutest whims of the early autumn winds. From our kitchen, I watched the branches of a downy birch tree and knew my winnowing moment had come. Soon after that, I learnt to interpret the different shapes the airborne chaff made – the curls, twirls, wreathes and scarves of yellow and gold. I also loved how I became gilded in chaff, from cap to boot. Back in the house, I left a trail of coppery dust from room to room, like breadcrumbs through the forest in the fairy tale of Hansel and Gretel. I also loved the soundtrack of winnowing, particularly the hiss of grain in the basket when I was panning from side to side. It was like a jazz drum loop played with brushes.

I winnowed the emmer faster than the Hen Gymro, but only because threshing the emmer, with its extra layers of protective hulls or glumes, had been such an exhausting process. The ancient Egyptians moistened the spikelets with a little water and pounded them with heavy wooden pestles in limestone mortars. Other civilizations parched emmer spikelets with fire, before pounding them in mortars. I tried both methods, but in a granite pestle and mortar. It didn't work – too many grains were shattered. Then a friend, Mick Petts, lent me an old cast-iron tabletop manual grinder. On his advice, I glued a piece of tractor inner tube to one of the grinding plates. To my astonishment, it worked. At least, it worked better than the pestle and mortar. The process involved sifting and was very slow, but the emmer grains were finally freed. As the emmer hulls make excellent bedding, I saved a sack for my neighbour who keeps ponies. The straw from both varieties of wheat was too short and uneven to be used as roof thatching. Instead, I spread it as mulch around the young trees we have planted at home.

The winnowed grain was piling into sacks, but it was obvious I did not need a silo to store it. I hardly needed a dustbin. The yield, particularly set against my expectations and my labours, had been poor. Almost everything that could have gone wrong, had gone wrong. The field had flooded. The rabbits along the railway line had enjoyed epicurean feasts. There had even been a drought – in Wales! The growing season across the UK was 'a disaster for everyone', according to Ed Dickin. Nick Powell described his harvest as 'the worst ever', though I had heard Nick say that before. I was beginning to understand how the great variation in wheat yields from one year to the next was a common experience of all farmers, in all ages. Even so, my ineptitude as a farmer, albeit one practising Neolithic husbandry, had been laid bare. I estimated I would have around 100kg of grain. I had anticipated several times that. I would, at least, have enough flour to make bread at home for a year. But if I had been a Bronze Age farmer in the Black Mountains, a fourteenth-century serf, or even a peasant farmer during the agricultural depression at the end of the nineteenth century, a crop failure on this scale would have meant disaster.

Nonetheless, every time I thrust a hand into one of the sacks and stirred the berries, listening for the crackle,

checking the grain was sufficiently dry, I felt a pulse of satisfaction. The berries – the emmer and the Hen Gymro – were
smaller than they might have been because of the drought,
but I had grown them. Occasionally, I pulled a few grains out
and rolled them across the palm of my hand. They were desiccated, hard and minutely different in myriad ways. The hues
of brown ranged from almond and camel to auburn and umber
via cinnamon, caramel and cocoa. I thought of William Blake
and his 'grain of sand' in *Auguries of Innocence*. Perhaps a grain
of wheat would have been a better metaphor. I was, in a sense,
holding 'infinity' in the palm of my hand. The long history
of emmer wheat is contained in a single grain. If I took just
one shrivelled seed and cultivated it carefully, I would have a
handful of wheat next year. If I kept on re-planting it all, there
would be acres of wheat in a decade. In a century, you could
feed a nation. The genetic material in these grains could, hypo-
thetically, be feeding the human race millennia from now.
Alternatively, I reasoned, I could just take it all to the mill and
be making bread next week.

smithereens of detritus that I had failed to winnow out accumulated underneath the cleaner in a tray. The grain pattered into a heavy paper sack to the side. When my wheat had been through the machine twice, Andrew's wife, Anne, arrived. She would carry out the all-important assessment, to determine whether my grain was good enough to mill.

Long before Anne became a miller, she was a cereal pathologist. She has a degree in microbiology and a PhD on disease resistance mechanisms in oats. She worked at the Welsh Plant Breeding Station, the institution that first collected samples of Hen Gymro in the 1920s, the same Hen Gymro that I had eventually planted. That is the blessed thing about life in a small country like Wales – all our stories are woven together.

Anne thrust the metal prongs of a grain moisture meter into the sack of Hen Gymro. Her lips pursed, waiting for the digital reading: 'Sixteen per cent, that's acceptable,' she said. With a plastic tub, she scooped out a pint of seeds and held it up to the light, studying the grain. Her fingers riffled across the surface, disturbing the seeds. Intermittently, she spooned a dozen seeds into her palm and flicked at them with a thumbnail.

Occasionally Anne raised the tub, smelling the grain. Nutty and fishy smells indicate infection from diseases like fusarium, bunt and ergot, she explained. The latter is serious for humans. A fungal infection, ergot causes 'ergotism' in humans, a form of poisoning with symptoms including nausea, seizures and hallucinations. Also known as 'St Anthony's Fire' or 'Dancing Mania', outbreaks of ergotism during the Middle Ages in Europe caused mass hysteria and death. In 944, 40,000 people died in the Limoges district of France alone. Over centuries, outbreaks of ergotism wove their way into our collective folk memory and even, it has been suggested, evoked medieval ideas about witchcraft. Anne was also looking for insect damage, lost embryos, sprouted grains and any broken seeds that had sneaked through the cleaning machine. There were a plethora of reasons why a miller might reject my grain. Anne knew most of them.

This was the first time I had shown my grain to anyone. My wife had lost interest when the first flail broke. I hadn't dared show my meagre sacks to Nick Powell, who sends plump seeds by the containerload to industrial millers. Had I been hiding subconsciously from the truth? What if my wheat grain was diseased or deformed? It was entirely within Anne's power to refuse to mill it. In a single sentence, she could crush my hopes and end my project to make bread to feed my family, here, now.

Andrew and Anne Parry never intended to become flour millers. In 2006, they bought a cottage on the River Wyre in Llanrhystud, a small village in West Wales set back from a shingle beach facing the southern, grey tail of the Irish Sea. Andrew, a musician in his youth, was then working as a network computer manager. Anne had received funding for a research fellowship ('highly technical stuff, on powdery mildew,' she said) and they had seven children to raise. Life was up to the gunwales.

'The cottage just happened to have a mechanically derelict but physically intact mill next door,' Andrew explained, opening up the 'tun', the wooden casement around the millstones, to clean out the last of the flour from the previous milling. 'Even though the weir was broken, the millstream was full of debris and the waterwheel hadn't turned seriously since the 1950s, everything somehow looked like it wanted to work.' Wheel by wheel, cog by cog, and stone by stone, they brought the mill back to life. Walls had to be repaired and lime-pointed, oak uprights were installed for structural integrity and floors rebuilt. In 2008, the waterwheel turned for the first time in half a century; in 2009, the Parrys milled flour.

'Where were we? Oh, yes, your grain,' Anne said, knocking the dustpan and brush together. She studied me over her glasses for a moment, flicking white hair from her elfin eyes. She had put the Hen Gymro down, while she swept out the tun. 'This is a really nice sample, actually. There is still the odd weed seed, but the dust has gone. The cleaner has polished it up. The grain looks small, but only in comparison to modern wheats. As we deal in old varieties, it doesn't look small to us. In fact, it looks great.'

Phew.

'See how some of the grain looks flinty, almost like stone,' Anne said. 'Millers love this, and it's mixed with some softer seeds too. A balance like this often makes for a good baking wheat. I think we're ready to mill. Shall we get some water?'

Botanically, a grain of wheat is a fruit. To be more precise, it is a 'caryopsis' – a dry indehiscent fruit with an outer layer or 'pericarp' that is fused with the thin seed coat or 'testa'. The caryopsis is characteristic of the Poaceae grass family, to which wheat belongs. A grain has a dorsal (back) and a ventral (front) side, as well as a top and a bottom. The front has a crease, and minute hairs sprout from the top. Each grain comprises three

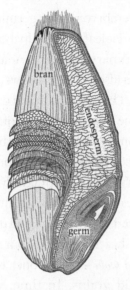

parts called 'bran', 'endosperm' and 'germ'. The bran has a complicated structure consisting of several outer layers, including a tough skin that protects the seed from organisms in the soil, inner coats that control the intake of water, and the aleurone layer, which is particularly rich in nutrients including minerals, vitamins, phenolic antioxidants and lignans that are all useful during initial seed development. The bulkiest part of the grain, around 75 to 80 per cent, is the endosperm, a larder of energy for the growing seedling until it develops roots. The endosperm is composed of small amounts of vitamins and minerals, traces of storage proteins and a large proportion of carbohydrates, in the form of starch. The third part is the germ, which contains the plant embryo and typically accounts for 2–3 per cent of the grain's dry weight. The embryo consists of a scutellum that secretes enzymes to dissolve the endosperm starch and feed the embryo during germination, a coleoptile that grows into the first leaf on germination, and a coleorhiza that encloses the primary root. Essential fatty acids and B vitamins in the germ also provide a powerful package for the seedling in early life. The proportion and organization of these three parts determine the hardness or softness of a kernel.

Milling cereal grains – breaking open the tough, outer shell so our digestive juices can get to work on the germ and the endosperm – is man's oldest, continuously practised industry. No other single thread of technological human food production is so closely paired to our ascent (and descent) as a species. At first, we used the shearing power of our molar teeth ('molar' from the Latin word *mola* – a millstone), to unlock the nourishing value of wild grains. In time, we perceived that pre-grinding between two rough stones not only reduced wear on our teeth, it also produced more palatable food for less effort. Possibly as long as 45,000 years ago, we started to shape roundish stones with flat working surfaces for grinding. At roughly the same time, we developed the pestle and mortar for pounding. During the Magdalenian, the last great culture of the Upper Palaeolithic that flourished across Europe 15,000 to 9,000 years ago, flat-ish grinding stones were paired and shaped for specific purposes.

The archaeological site of Tell Abu Hureyra, in the Euphrates valley of modern Syria, produced an abundance of these basic grinding stones. The site was occupied twice. Debris accumulated during the second occupation, 9,000 to 7,000 years ago, when agriculture was widely practised in the region, includes the bones of 162 people. These people appear to have lived healthily, though some, particularly women and young girls, suffered from collapsed vertebrae in the lower back and arthritic big toes – the consequence, it is thought, of long hours on their knees, grinding grain using 'saddle stones'.

Also known as 'saddle querns', or 'metates' in Central America, saddle stones were the favoured milling tool of nearly all early agricultural peoples, from the Indus River to Arizona. The user knelt at one end of the lower, usually oblong, stone, and controlled the movement of the upper stone, which was more like a rolling pin than a pounder, back and forth with two hands. As the skeletons at Tell Abu Hureyra attest, using a saddle stone was hard work. Archaeologists have estimated that it took two hours to grind the daily flour intake for one adult on a saddle stone. This Sisyphean chore commonly fell to slave women. When the biblical character Samson was blinded and chained up by the Philistines, he was further humiliated by being made to grind grain on a saddle stone.

Around 400 BC, rotary motion was applied to grinding, replacing the reciprocating motion of saddle stones. This abrupt and brilliant intellectual leap, one that probably took place simultaneously in several places, led to the 'rotary quern' – a device with two circular stones, one static, the other rotating with a central pivot, turned by a crank handle and fitted together with a slight conical shape towards the centre of the grinding surfaces. Almost as soon as the rotary system was adopted, animal power was utilized. Output increased greatly and milling became a commercial activity. Rotary motion would, in time, make it possible to apply non-organic power to a myriad tasks that man, with his limited strength, water-powered sawmills meant wood and marble could be cut faster and with greater precision than ever before; yet more Vitruvian mechanisms fulled cloth and drove ironworks. Centuries later, the watermill was described as 'the mother of modern industry'. For Lynn White Jr, the historian and author of the influential 1967 article 'The Historical Roots of our Ecologic Crisis' (where he argued that the Judeo-Christian tradition nurtured our exploitative attitude to nature), the industrial revolution – and our current environmental crisis – started when humans first used the power of water in industrial processes other than milling.

Though the records are scant, it is highly likely the Romans introduced watermills to Britain. By the time of the Domesday Book in 1086, there were 5,624 mills south of the River Trent – a huge number, one for every five square miles in several counties, and evidence that driving millstones now underpinned economic and social power. Throughout the Middle Ages, lords of estates and religious houses monopolized the highly profitable milling trade. They built their own watermills (and later, on the lowlands, using technology that originated in the Near East, windmills) in order to establish exclusive franchises. The miller was an employee of the lord and the fee for milling was levied in grain. In France, the church traditionally owned all the rivers, and the mills too.

Felin Ganol ('Middle Mill' in Welsh) was one of three mills on the River Wyre and part of the Moelifor estate. Owned by the Gwynn family, the estate dates back to the time of the Welsh Princes in the High Middle Ages. When the estate was broken up in the 1880s, the tenants bought the mill.

paper separates them. Ideally, the stones should grip a piece of brown paper at the eye, a piece of newspaper halfway, and a piece of tissue paper at the edge.

'Be careful not to get anything caught in the mechanism,' Andrew said, with raised, white eyebrows, as I leant over to study the spur wheel. 'The mill won't stop for you. It'd be easy enough to lose a finger or two.'

Anne had already poured the Hen Gymro grain into the hopper. It was falling via a wooden chute called a 'shoe' into the 'eye of the stone'. The stones were grinding away. Flour was beginning to fall out of the tun, into a paper sack on the level below us. Anne darted downstairs, light on her feet, caught a cup of flour in a plastic tub and skipped back up. She ran a handful of the brown flour through her fingers, plying it softly, as you might test the quality of silk. The flour was too coarse, she declared. Andrew went out to adjust the sluice. The artistry in milling good flour, Anne explained, is finding the balance between the amount of water (and the speed the stones are turning), the gap between the stones and the flow of grain. The formula changes for every variety of wheat and even different husbandry techniques. It also changes every day, because of fluctuating humidity levels. Finally, it can change while you are milling, as the stones warm up.

When the Parrys started milling, it was difficult to source local wheat. The perception, Anne explained as she adjusted the space between the stones with the 'tentering arm', was that you couldn't grow good milling wheat in Wales. But Andrew and Anne had read Felin Ganol's historic ledgers, held in the Welsh National Archive: they knew it was possible.

Steadily, because that's how Welsh farmers do things, good milling wheats are being re-introduced and grown on a small scale, in various parts of the country. Local grain economies are quietly beginning to stir again.

'With organic, heritage varieties, yields tend to be low, but the bread tastes really good,' Anne said, coming back up the stairs with another tub of flour. She kept raising the tub and sniffing. If the stones are too close together, or there is not enough grain going through, the millstones become too hot, she explained, ruining the flour and even damaging the stones. The idiom 'nose to the grindstone', I was reminded, most likely refers to millers who frequently leant close to their stones, to check they were not overheating.

'This smells fine at the moment. I'm going to increase the flow of grain slightly and bring the stones closer. It's still a little coarse, but we're working our way down to the right fineness. Here, you have a smell. It's your flour,' she said.

The mechanism of the mill had reached a good tempo now. The creeks, dinks, bonks and donks, overlaid by the sound of tumbling water, created a rhythmic, soothing noise, like a locomotive chuffing into the night: 'The rush of water, and the booming of the mill, bring a dreamy deafness,' George Eliot wrote in *Mill on the Floss*. By counting the knocks of the spindle on the 'damsel' – the device that strikes the shoe to release grain, so-called because it chatters away all day – Andrew calculated the millstone was turning at 60 revolutions per minute.

'This is slow or "cold" milling. It's traditional in France,' he said. 'Some mills turn at 120 rpm, but we won't demonstrate that now, if you don't mind. The whole building shakes at that speed.'

Andrew 'dresses' or cuts the furrows in the stones himself. Two hundred years ago, millstones were commonly dressed by travelling craftsmen called 'millwrights'. Over time, miniscule shards of metal, or 'mettle', embedded themselves into the lower arms of practised millwrights, leaving a blue tinge on their skin. Millers would then check their hands, to know if they were versed in the job.

'It's where the phrase "to test someone's mettle" comes from. Amazing how many turns of phrase come from this one industry,' Andrew said. 'For centuries, debate has raged over the best patterns and furrow profiles. Our stones are cut to a traditional "harp pattern", but there are different patterns for different cereals and, inevitably, a huge number of regional variations. It goes on and on. If you want to find out more, Rob, there's a whole afternoon of boredom in store for you.'

A well-dressed stone is fundamental to milling good flour, though. As the top stone turns, the edges of the furrows split and slice the grain progressively, working like scissors, producing flakes of bran. The bulky endosperm is, in turn, crushed and ground into powdery flour as it shifts with centrifugal force towards the periphery or 'skirt', across the flat spaces on the stones (called 'lands') between the grooves. In this process, the minute germ of the seed gets squashed and blended into the powdered endosperm.

The product of stone grinding between millstones was historically called 'meal', as in 'wholemeal', Anne told me. The word 'flour', derived from the French *fleur*, literally meaning

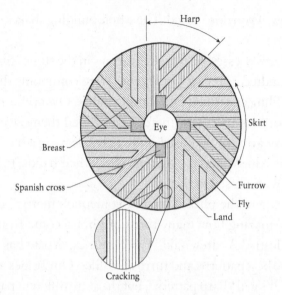

Cracking

'flower' or 'blossom', and metaphorically meaning 'the finest', formerly referred only to refined meal – white flour that had been sifted or 'bolted' to remove the bran flakes and the largest starchy particles of endosperm (called 'semolina') that had not been crushed into fine powder between the stones.

'We're getting quite a lot of bran,' Anne added, coming back up the stairs with another tub of meal. 'Because the Hen Gymro grains are small, there is a relatively high proportion of bran to endosperm. The flour itself is pretty fine, though. If you want to sift your meal to remove the bran, we have a mechanical sieving box downstairs. It dates from the mid-1800s but it's been restored. It's basically a cylinder with graded meshes. That's how you get different grades of white flour. Do you want white flour?'

For a large part of human history, certainly from ancient Greece until the end of the nineteenth century, the whiteness of bread was a signifier of class. Gods, angels, kings, queens, aristocrats, the *haut monde* and anyone else with money to burn (the 'upper crust', you might say) ate the whitest bread made from wheat flour. Servants, slaves, plebs, the poor, the oppressed, Christian ascetics and, presumably, writers, on the other hand, filled their stomachs with the darkest, coarsest brown loaves made from a variety of wholegrains including wheat, rye and barley. White for the wealthy, brown for the downtrodden and, as the Roman satirist Juvenal wrote, 'Don't forget the colour of your own bread.'

Knowing what we now know about the superior nutritional benefits of wholemeal bread that has been properly fermented, it is difficult to understand why the partiality for white over brown endured for so long. If anything, it ought to be the other way around. It is one of the great paradoxes in the story of food. Some historians have suggested the preference related to colour – whiteness has always symbolized cleanliness and purity. Others have wondered if it was the baking qualities of white flour that originally entranced high society. Dough made with sifted flour rises better, producing airier loaves with greater volume (and, importantly, fewer impurities like dirt, grit, straw and even, according to some accounts, rodent faeces) than loaves made with wholemeal. Of course, there is also the matter of taste: as my kids kept telling me, white bread is sweeter than dark or brown bread. This is because it has a higher proportion of starch that is readily converted to sugar by enzymes in human saliva. White bread is also generally softer in texture and easier to chew, leaving teeth intact and putting paid to the old Italian proverb: 'He that has teeth has not bread, he that has bread has not teeth.' One more hypothesis is that this predilection was founded on socioeconomic grounds – producing white flour was time-consuming for the miller, which made white bread more expensive and, such is human folly, thereby more desirable. Until the Industrial Revolution, eating white bread was an act of everyday conspicuous consumption, rather like eating wholemeal sourdough bread from an artisan bakery today. For Andy Forbes, the partiality endured for a simpler reason: brown loaves for the proletariat were made with whatever flour was left, after the finest white had been sifted out.

Whatever the origins of the preference, the consensus of scientific, medical and epicurean opinion – that bread made from white flour was both better to eat and better for us – held for millennia. As long ago as the fourth century BC, Archestratus, a Greek poet and possibly the world's first gourmand, wrote that 'cleanly bolted' flour from the island of Lesbos was so white, the gods should send Hermes to buy it for them. In the third century AD, the Egyptian philosopher Athenaeus listed dozens of different kinds of bread, noting that the rich favoured white bread made from wheat. By the fourteenth century, there were different kinds of bread for almost every distinct social echelon in France, from *pain de chevalier* to *pain de valet*. These breads started out white and became darker and coarser the lower the rank. Gervase Markham provided a rare glimpse of English bread recipes from the early modern period in his book *The English Huswife*, published in 1615. His recipe for farm workers' bread included a mix of minimally sifted wheat, rye, barley and dried pea flour. It is telling that Markham, a famous horse-breeder, also insisted that leavened bread made from the finest white flour be fed to elite race horses.

Long before the invention of the mechanical sieving box or 'flour dresser', during the Industrial Revolution, millers sifted meal by hand, in a variety of homemade riddles, sieves, screens and strainers. The Egyptians used papyrus, rushes and horsehair. The Greeks and Romans devised sieves made of finely woven linen and cotton cloths, to produce multiple grades of flour. The Normans used fine-hair sieves. Canvas and woollen fabrics were also used in the Middle Ages. Improvements in weaving in the mid-eighteenth century introduced silk gauze to the sifting process. This made white flour, for those who could afford it, even finer still.

Until the late nineteenth century, however, no amount of bolting could extract the germ from stoneground flour. As Anne explained, the germ that contains the plant embryo gets crushed between the stones along with the endosperm, releasing a suite of nutrients and natural oils that contribute significantly to the flavour and aroma of baked bread. These oils also turn flour rancid, which limits its shelf life. Thus, from the time of the Norman Conquest until the mid-1800s, mills were as common in Britain as supermarkets are today.

'Around 150 years ago, there were 400 mills in this county, Ceredigion. There were four in this village alone,' Anne said. 'Because the oils in the germ oxidize, stoneground flour eventually goes off, so farmers would visit the mill ten or more times a year, to grind small batches of grain. There are many variables, like the type of grain, the amount of germ and storage conditions, so it's difficult to say exactly how long your flour will last. Cold-milled heritage wheats do last longer, though. If you store the flour in a cool, dry place, it'll be fine to bake with for at least six months. I've baked with eighteen-month-old flour, and it was fine.'

What happens to flour after it has been milled is complicated, Andy Forbes had previously explained to me. For the first twenty-four hours, the level of enzyme activity makes it particularly 'lively', while it also has good 'volume'. After this, 'strength' tails off until, at around two and a half to three weeks post milling, flour starts to 'age' – it becomes stronger again (and whiter), due to oxidization, but less lively. 'Aged' flour is preferred in urban French baguette baking.

Knowing that wholemeal flour can go off, I had brought less than half my grain to Felin Ganol. I would either return to Llanrhystud again, or borrow my neighbour's electric countertop mill, to produce fresh flour every time I baked. The resurgence of interest in locally grown grain in many parts of the world has been facilitated by these small-scale, domestic mills. My neighbour bought his twenty years ago in Germany, a country that values the enzymatic oomph of freshly ground, wholemeal flour more than anywhere else in Europe. In fact, Germans eat more bread per capita than anyone else in Europe, while they have over 3,000 different types of bread. Germany's diverse bread culture today is heavily influenced by *Lebensreform* ('life reform'), the back-to-the-land social movement of the late nineteenth and early twentieth centuries that celebrated wholemeal breads as a source of health. Dense breads made from unrefined meal like *Vollkornbrot* (wholemeal seeded bread) and *Roggenmischbrot* (wheat and rye), both common in medieval times, were revived. They remain important in German bread culture today.

The apparatus for milling wheat between pairs of steel rollers rather than stone wheels was devised in the mid-nineteenth century, partly to address the issue of rancid flour. It was the most significant advance in milling cereals since the Vitruvian watermill in the first century BC. The development of the 'roller mill' began in Switzerland in the 1830s with a young engineer, Jacob Sulzberger, before reaching Britain, Germany and then Hungary, where a succession of small inventions improved the technology.

In 1873, a group of American millers on a tour of Europe visited Vienna, then a focal point of baking excellence, to attend the 'World Exposition'. Having tasted a range of *pâtisseries viennoises* in the elegant Habsburg surroundings, the millers inevitably enquired how the fine white flour was produced. Five years later, when the famous Washburn Mill in Minneapolis (then known as 'Flour City') was destroyed by a 'flour bomb' explosion, the proprietor, Cadwallader C. Washburn, recruited Hungarian engineers to rebuild it. America's first state-of-the-art steel roller mill arose from the debris. The newfangled machinery proved to be particularly effective at milling the hard red spring and winter wheats being grown at scale on the Great Plains of the USA and the Canadian Prairies. Steel roller mills then spread rapidly, as towns like Milwaukee, Omaha and Des Moines awoke to find themselves fledged as cities based around the milling industry.

Roller mills comprise a series of fluted rollers, arranged in pairs with incrementally smaller gaps, as well as a sophisticated arrangement of sieves. The first sets of rollers, called 'break rolls', shear or scalp the kernels. The white endosperm particles are then processed to uniform size, through a series of 'reduction rolls', producing several flour streams with different qualities and degrees of fineness. Crucially, all the bran and the entire germ are extracted early on in the process, and streamed separately.

This new system of milling offered several advantages over traditional stone grinding. The machinery was fast, efficient and easy to maintain. Paramount, because the germ and the fatty oils contained in it could be readily separated from the endosperm, the flour no longer went off within a few months of being milled. For the first time, flour became a stable, predictable commodity with a long shelf life. It could be distributed to grocery stores all over the country, where it sat in packets on shelves. It could be bought in bulk by bakeries with longer distribution chains. It could even be exported around the world. Steel roller mills grew in capacity, as both the milling industry and the flour trade expanded, before consolidating into fewer and fewer hands. Watermills and windmills, an integral part of highly localized food economies wherever cereals had been grown for a thousand years, began to disappear fast.

Large-scale bakeries were particularly delighted with the new style of flour. It was cheaper. It was more reliable. It gave bakers more control. The bread was softer, easier to eat and denser with energy. And, once the millers started to add bleaching agents like chlorine and nitrogen peroxide to flour, the bread was whiter than anything the world had ever seen. Towards the end of the nineteenth century, as vast numbers of European peasantry moved into cities to fire the furnaces of the Industrial Revolution, a great democratization of taste took place. The whitest bread made from refined flour, a prerogative of the rich (and their race horses) since antiquity, became available to the masses for the first time. There was one problem, though – this 'modern bread' was nutritionally worthless.

In removing the bran and the germ to facilitate flour production, millers inadvertently extracted or depleted a wide range of vitamins, minerals and micronutrients naturally present in wheat. These include vitamins E and K, folate, iron, thiamine, riboflavin, niacin, calcium, magnesium, sodium, phosphorus, potassium, cobalt, zinc, copper, manganese, selenium and omega-3 fatty acids, all of which contribute to a balanced human diet. The dietary fibre in bran is also hugely important; it feeds the intestinal biota when it passes through the human gut and helps prevent constipation. Epidemiological studies in the last fifteen years have consistently shown that eating wholemeal bread – in fact, eating wholegrain foods in general – lowers cholesterol and reduces the risk of coronary heart disease, stroke, hypertension, bowel cancer and Type 2 diabetes, among other common illnesses. People who eat plenty of wholegrain foods weigh less and live longer, with less disease, than people who don't. Or, as the early twentieth-century refrain of the American wholemeal-bread movement put it: 'The whiter your bread, the sooner you're dead.'

For writer Michael Pollan, the high priest of American gour-
mands and an Archestratus for our dystopian age, the introduction
of roller milling is a critical turning point not just for good bread,
but for food. He believes the industrial production of pure white
flour in the second half of the nineteenth century is the moment
when civilization first began processing food in a way that made
it not only less nutritious, but detrimental to our health and
well-being. As Pollan writes in *Cooked: A Natural History of
Transformation*: 'The quest for an ever-whiter shade of bread,
which goes all the way back to the Greeks and Romans, is a
parable about the folly of human ingenuity – about how our
species can sometimes be too smart for its own good.'

The introduction of roller milling did not in itself initiate
the wholemeal-bread movement. There had been a handful
of enlightened proselytizers, generally lone voices, advocating
the health benefits of eating all parts of the wheat grain, prior
to this. The Reverend Sylvester Graham, dubbed the 'prophet
of bran bread' by Ralph Waldo Emerson, was an American
Presbyterian minister and social reformer who found fame in
the 1830s. He promoted a complete health regimen that
included hard mattresses, cold showers, abstaining from alcohol, restricted masturbation, and a diet of fruit, vegetables
and bread made from coarsely ground, unsifted wheat flour.
Earlier still, during the French Revolution, the Convention
in Paris under Robespierre ordered, in 1793, that only one
type of bread be made throughout the country. *Pain d'égalité*
included 25 per cent rye flour and 75 per cent unsifted, bran-
heavy wheat flour. The noble idea was that all classes should
eat the same, healthy bread. In the event, they all despised it

equally and it was quickly forgotten. The inherent preference for white bread in France was too strong. It still is.

Long before this, Plato briefly considered the question of wholemeal bread in *The Republic*, written in 380 BC. He concluded that in the ideal *polis* or city-state, people would eat rough country breads made from wholemeal barley and wheat flour: 'And with such a diet they may be expected to live in peace and health to a good age.' In the Roman novel *The Satyricon* the author Petronius sneers at a guest at Trimalchio's feast who asks for brown bread: 'We had whole-wheat bread,' the guest explains, 'which I'd rather have than white, because it puts strength into you, and when I take a crap afterwards, I don't have to yell.'

The coming of steel roller mills, however, prompted a concerted and energetic backlash against refined white flour for the first time in history. In 1880, May Yates, an artist, sanitary campaigner and rousing public speaker, sold her own jewellery in order to found the Bread Reform League in London. The organization promoted wholemeal bread, specifically to improve nutrition among the urban poor. There were already outbreaks of illnesses caused, Yates argued, by deficiencies of nutrients ordinarily found in wholemeal bread. With the cry of 'Brown is best', Yates championed the case for wholemeal across Europe and the USA for thirty years.

Dr Thomas Allinson took the campaigning work of the Bread Reform League a step further. In 1892, he bought a stonemill in Bethnal Green, East London. He then established a bakery to produce his own range of breads. 'The true staff of life is wholemeal bread,' he declared. Allinson was a controversial figure, though. He publicly opposed the use of drugs in medicine and his licence to practise as a doctor was revoked in 1892. He also mixed his passion for brown bread with calls for wider social and political reforms. He was a friend of Gandhi, a legal student in London in the late 1880s, and the Mahatma remained a critic of refined white flour his entire life. The Allinson brand is extant today. British teenagers of the 1980s like me cannot forget the award-winning advert that launched the Allinson tag-line, 'Bread's better wi' nowt taken out'. The brand is now part of a vast, international food industry conglomerate, and the industrial bread made in Allinson's name must have the doctor spinning like a fluted steel roller in his grave.

In 1909, the Bread Reform League proposed that an official minimum 'standard' for bread, made from 'unadulterated wheat flour, containing at least 80 per cent of the wheat kernel, including the germ' be adopted nationally. The campaign for 'Standard Bread', backed by the *Daily Mail* newspaper, had some success. Home baking came back into fashion, briefly. Millers and bakers began to comply with the League's demands. In 1911, several prominent medical men including Sir Frederick Gowland Hopkins, the biochemist and future Nobel Prize winner, concurred that Standard Bread contained as yet 'unrecognized food substances' that were vital for the human metabolism to function well. A year later, these substances were given a name – 'vitamins'.

During the early decades of the twentieth century, authorities in industrialized countries could hardly ignore the links between white flour, nutritional deficiencies and the emergence of new public health issues. Urban populations that relied entirely upon modern bread experienced increases in both Type 2 diabetes and heart disease. There were also epidemics of mysterious diseases, later identified as beriberi and pellagra – caused, respectively, by deficiencies in vitamins B1 (thiamine) and B3 (niacin). During the First World War, the British government did pass legislation regulating the extraction rates of wheat flour. In 1916, commercial bakers were forced to use 'Standard Flour', which contained more bran and germ, in the production of 'War Bread'. They were temporary victories, though.

Wonder Bread, the iconic brand of double-bleached, sugar-dense sliced white bread, hit American shops in 1921. The new loaf was presented to the public as some sort of modern miracle food. Actually, it was processed junk. By the 1930s, industrial white bread had almost completely prevailed in both Britain and the USA. As Andrew Whitley wrote in *Bread Matters*, 'The millers and bakers fought tooth and nail against the scientific consensus in the 1930s that roller milling had removed so many nutrients from flour that many people, especially the poor, were subsisting on considerably less than was physiologically required.' The once urgent debate – the 'war on white' – that had begun a century earlier with Sylvester Graham, quietly petered out. A phenomenal economic, cultural and dietary shift had taken place in the developed world, to the detriment of health on a societal level. To compound the idiocy, millers were by this time selling the bran and the germ – the most nutritious 25 per cent of the seed containing vitamins, antioxidants, essential oils and minerals – either to the pharmaceutical industry or to farms, as animal feed.

Wholemeal bread did return to the national diet during the Second World War in Britain. The Ministry of Food wanted to ensure the population received the optimal nutritional value from the flour that was shipped, in perilous conditions, across the Atlantic from Canada. The National Loaf, made from unbleached flour with only the coarsest bran extracted, was created in 1942. It was grey, dry, widely despised and nick-named 'Hitler's Secret Weapon'. The commercial production of sliced, pure white bread was banned from 1942 until 1950, but when the restriction was lifted, the National Loaf was largely abandoned.

Governments on both sides of the Atlantic began to re-constitute flour under wartime health measures with calcium first, and then a variety of vitamins and other nutrients natur-ally present in wheat, and which the roller milling process had just removed. In Britain, calcium (in the form of chalk) was added back to flour by law from 1942, to prevent rickets. Iron, thiamine and niacin were added from 1953, although in lower amounts than existed naturally in the wheat seed. In the USA, the new procedure was called 'enrichment' – with-out irony.

By the 1960s, the white flour industrial complex was unas-sailable. The hippies stood far enough back to appreciate the insanity of a system that bound millers to put back a handful of the nutrients they had just gone to great lengths to remove. Home baking with wholemeal flour emerged as an important part of the protest by radical young people, against the commercialization of daily life. This was the first serious opposition to industrialized bread for almost half a century. White bread became a symbol of the failings of not just the food-processing industry, but of western civilization: 'Don't eat white – eat right and fight,' hippies chanted. Wholemeal flour and brown bread were celebrated again, albeit by a small part of society. While baking wholemeal bread was partly about reclaiming the flavours of a pre-industrialized food system, it was also a political act.

The germ of this renaissance in brown bread was the now iconic *Tassajara Bread Book*. Written in the late 1960s by Edward Espe Brown, a student of Zen Buddhism in California, it began: 'Dedicated with respect and appreciation to all my teachers past, present and future; gods, men and demons; beings animate and inanimate, living and dead, alive and dying. Rock and water, wind and tree, bread dough rising Vastly all are patient with me.' Far out. The first print run sold out immediately. There are an estimated 750,000 copies in circulation today. For many, it remains the bible of bread baking.

'Yes, of course I had a copy of *The Tassajara Bread Book*,' Anne said. 'We all did – all these bearded folks running around Mid Wales in the 1970s with their copies. I remember it vividly. Lots of people left London and bought smallholdings here then. The bread we made tasted great, but it was very, very heavy. I suppose that was the beginning of the slow resurgence of interest in real bread, the same resurgence that we feel part of now.'

As the last of the Hen Gymro emptied out of the hopper, we poured in my emmer grain. Anne had never milled emmer before. She hunched her shoulders and arched her eyebrows in mock, girlish excitement. Andrew was outside, adjusting the water again. Anne danced up and down the stairs, gathering emmer flour in her tub from the wooden chute.

'The flour is lovely,' she said. 'If the grain goes through the stones too quickly, it can be gritty or sandy, but this has a really nice texture, nicer than I anticipated. The bran is very fragile or brittle, and it has broken into tiny pieces. It's different from the flaky Hen Gymro. Have a feel. You did this!'

I dug my fingers in and scooped out a palmful of the nutmeg-coloured flour. It was a bit like atta, a wholegrain flour used to make chapattis and parathas in India that my mum used to buy. The stones were warm now and the flour emitted a complex aroma – hazelnuts, fresh grass, the earth, the smell of rolling in a field when I was a kid with my brother, playing Cowboys and Indians. The visible flecks of bran crowned the miniature dune in my palm. The flour poured like fine, dry soil through my fingers back into the tub. Anne was right. It did have a nice texture.

'We won't add anything to your flour,' Andrew said, coming over to inspect the hopper, with a wink. 'Millers get a bad enough rap as it is.'

I was not concerned – they were both far too decent – but Andrew was right. Unscrupulous millers have been adulterating wheat flour with cheaper, less wholesome ingredients for millennia. Pliny the Elder (23–79 AD) noted how emmer flour was augmented with chalk. During medieval times, millers reputedly adulterated flour with an extraordinary host of additives to bulk it up or whiten it, including beanmeal, beechnuts, chestnuts, sawdust, sand, potato flour, chalk, slaked lime, plaster of Paris, pipe clay and even the ash of ground-up bones. In the fourteenth century, Geoffrey Chaucer crystallized the public revulsion at millers in his opus *The Canterbury Tales*. The Miller of the story is not only a physically grotesque and uncouth character (with a large hairy wart on the end of his nose), he is also so dishonest he has a 'thombe of gold' – an allusion to the English proverb, 'An honest miller hath a golden thumb.'

'There is a pub in Kent called The Honest Miller, presumably a reference to how rare they were,' Andrew said, before heading out of the door to adjust the water again.

In the eighteenth century, a London doctor, James Manning, campaigned obsessively against the adulteration of flour. It had got so bad, he claimed, 'bread, which has well been called the staff of life, becomes an arrow in the hand of death'. In Tobias Smollett's novel *The Expedition of Humphrey Clinker*, published in 1771, London bread is described as 'a deleterious paste, mixed with chalk, alum and bone-ashes'.

Anne and Andrew are not in the milling business to make money, though. They had been endlessly generous with their time and advice. Only reluctantly had they agreed to take a token fee for milling my grain. The mill, Andrew told me, had paid for its own restoration and it covers the upkeep, but it scarcely makes a profit. Generally, they mill on demand, producing a range of stoneground flours including locally grown wholemeal, spelt, rye, 'sieved white' and semolina, all of which are sold in shops and used by bakers across Wales.

'We're building steadily, as interest in old varieties of wheat grows. We currently mill about 1.5 tonnes a month – a tiny quantity compared to the major commercial operations. The mill is capable of up to two tonnes a week, if you milled morning, noon and night. Whether we would hold up is another matter.'

The light was fading inside the mill as the last of the emmer dripped from the hopper. Andrew stepped outside and stopped the water. The wheel eased and the great medieval mechanism of the mill juddered to a halt. Anne swept out the tun, gathering the remains of my emmer flour into the sack. I felt a pang of sadness. I had been looking forward to this day for so long and it was over. Lifting three sacks of flour into the car, though, a wave of renewed delight washed over me. I was taking home, over the darkening hills, forty kilos of high-quality flour – enough to bake loaves by the dozen.

'Have you baked with stoneground wholemeal flour before?' Anne asked. I admitted I had not. She briefly looked aghast. 'Ah, well. Good luck. Getting the dough to rise is a whole new ball game. You're going to bake some pancakes first.'

CHAPTER 5

Kneading Dreams: Leavening

'A little bread – a crust – a crumb –
A little trust – a demijohn –
Can keep the soul alive'
                                   – Emily Dickinson

'Meet Bernard, your new "mother",' my wife said, motioning
with her eyes to an old ice-cream pot on the kitchen table. I
was bemused. And cautious. Mrs Penn is a known prankster.
Not long after we were married, in the early days of internet
shopping, I bought a second-hand camera online for £1,200.
The vendor turned out to be living in Thailand, the parcel
was held up at UK Customs and my anxiety about being
ripped off filled the house like a noxious gas. When the parcel
finally arrived, my wife unpicked four layers of envelopes and
padding, replaced the £1,200 camera with another worth £12,
re-packaged it immaculately and presented it to me when I
got home. Then she watched with heavily restrained mirth as
I broke down at the kitchen table. That was one incident.
There have been others. I approached the ice-cream pot with
the care of a bomb disposal expert.

'Mother, *madre*, *levain*, leaven, Bernard – it goes by many
names. It is a natural starter, for baking sourdough bread. It's

alive and you need to feed it. Anyway. I'll leave you two to get to know each other,' she said. Bernard, it transpired, was a gift from a neighbour to whom my wife had expressed an interest in learning how to bake sourdough bread. I took the lid off. The contents looked like ceramic tile grouting. The uneven surface was covered in bubbles and scabs. The smell was sharp, acidic and unpleasant. I leant over the grey gloop, half expecting something to lurch out, like the creature bursting from John Hurt's chest in *Alien*. It was hard to believe this was, as I had read, the alchemical secret to one of the world's first and most important food-processing technologies – the transubstantiation of natural biomass into human nourishment in the form of bread.

That was seven years ago. I have since used Bernard to bake hundreds of loaves. I have also divided Bernard many times, and given tubs of starter to other initiates to the sourdough cult. To use a phrase overworked in the advertising industry, it's 'the gift that keeps on giving'. To my wife's list of names for sourdough starter, you could add 'sponge', 'batter', 'barm', *Sauerteig* (German), 'poolish', *chef* (French), *biga* (Italian), *pâte fermentée* (French), 'chief' or 'culture', among others. The many synonyms reflect the multitude of incrementally different ways the fermentation process has been used to leaven bread in diverse cultures.

A starter comprises flour and water. When mixed, the dough effectively captures an invisible cohort of naturally occurring wild yeasts and bacteria that multiply and ferment to establish a complex, living ecosystem. A single gram of starter might contain one billion bacteria cells and ten million wild yeast cells. If fed with more flour and water at regular intervals to revive fermentation, a starter can be kept alive for decades, or generations. In a few anecdotal cases, starters have survived for centuries. Andy Forbes, who helped me when I was planting my wheat, has a starter from a bakery on the island of Ischia, in the Gulf of Naples, which is supposed to date back to 1720.

Since inheriting Bernard, I have created two of my own starters from scratch. For the first one, I noted down a long list of often contradictory instructions from several baking books: sit a cut apple in water for three days then mix in the flour; start with rye flour (generally it has a high mineral content, which improves the flavour of many breads), then switch to wheat; add honey; don't add honey; feed it every twelve hours; feed it once a day; cover tightly; leave open; refrigerate; keep at room temperature of 18°C or lower for the whole evolution; add scored organic grapes; use potato water; only use bottled spring water. The list went on. I was confused. In the end, I mixed rye flour, water, honey and grapes. The process was exacting. Alarm clocks were constantly going off, prompting me to follow the next instruction. My children teased me for paying more attention to the welfare of my starter than to them. They had a point. When, after a few days, the starter finally came alive, generating gases and bubbling, my chest puffed up like a proud parent leaving the maternity ward. I called the starter 'Ivan' – the name, as my kids knew, I had always wanted to give to another son.

Before I began the next starter, I tore up the list of

instructions. I pinned a quote from Daniel Leader, a champion of real bread in America in the 1980s, above my desk: 'If I could convince you of just one thing about making bread, it would be how little effort it takes to cultivate a sourdough.' Honouring this, I left a mixture of our own Welsh spring water and my wholemeal flour in the kitchen. I measured nothing. When I remembered, I stirred and fed it. Occasionally, I discarded some. I had almost forgotten about it until, one warm afternoon, I caught a tangy whiff. I pulled the tub out from behind the biscuit tin. With minimal intervention, wild yeasts and bacteria had again taken up residence and organized themselves into an energetic, fermenting community. I named this starter 'Godisgoode', a medieval English term for 'barm' according to Elizabeth David in *English Bread and Yeast Cookery*. Barm is the yeasty foam that forms on the top of fermenting beer. It was commonly used to leaven bread from ancient Egyptian times until the modern era. 'Barm cake' is an extant term in the North of England for a soft, floury bread roll.

Starters evolve. The congregation of microorganisms shift like grains of sand on a beach, according to the foods they are given and the living conditions. The feeding regimen and the ambient temperature are the most important factors determining what microbes thrive or fail, influencing how bread tastes. Frequent feedings and warm temperatures generally favour yeasts, creating airier, milder-flavoured loaves. Infrequent meals and refrigeration favour the confederation of bacteria that help fashion a more acidic environment, leading to bread that is strongly flavoured with characteristic sourness.

Because I generally bake once a week, Bernard, Ivan and Godisgoode are taken out of the fridge and fed with roughly equal measures of water and flour every seven days. When I go on holiday, I neglect them. I do not ask our neighbours to pop in and feed them. They are starters, not cats. I certainly don't send them to a 'sourdough hotel' or 'sourdough-sitter', as obsessive 'bread heads' do. Nor do I ring my wife when I am away and drawl down the phone, 'Feed the bitch! . . . Feed the bitch or she'll die,' as Anthony Bourdain recalled one baker doing in *Kitchen Confidential.* Sometimes my starters need cajoling back to life with several feeds of rye flour when I have been absent, but they survive.

In my years of sourdough baking there has only been one setback, and that was human error. I once transferred Godisgoode to a small glass storage jar with a clip-top lid, while I washed the old tub out. At the same time, I fed all three starters. Absentmindedly, I closed the lid on the jar, left it in a warm kitchen and went for a long bike ride. When I came back, the intensity of the fermentation process, particularly the production of carbonic gas, had blown a piece of glass out of the jar wall.

Whoa. "Double, double toil and trouble, fire burn and cauldron bubble",' my wife said.

The event made me realize how little I understood about fermentation, yet all the baking books say it is the key to good bread. It improves the flavour, smell, touch, appearance, digestibility and, fundamentally, the nutritional value of wheat seeds. I wrestled with the notion of a process that requires the intimate cooperation of humans, plants and a host of unseen, living microorganisms thrown together in an ethereal dance of mutual exploitation. I asked a professional baker, who is a friend, when I might see a flicker of light at the end of the fermentation tunnel: 'Give it a decade,' he said, 'but start by understanding yeast. If there is magic in making bread, it is here.'

Wild yeast fermentation, the organic process in which sugars are metabolized by microscopic organisms, producing carbon dioxide and alcohol, was one of the first chemical reactions observed by humans on earth. In fact, our primate ancestors may well have been conscious of it before our species even evolved; it is likely yeasts have been fermenting ripe fruits ever since fruit trees first appeared on the planet, around 120 million years ago. We don't know when, but either apes or early humans discovered that the natural fermentation of fruit juices led to primitive forms of wine that were good to consume. At some point, probably in Mesopotamia or Egypt, certainly within the Fertile Crescent, we learnt to control this organic process, to advance the nascent arts of brewing and baking. It was a momentous step for the human race.

The ancient Egyptians and Mesopotamians did not know what yeasts were, of course. They couldn't even see them. A yeast cell is typically around four micrometres (0.004mm) in size. Nor did they understand ethanol fermentation. They simply chose to harness the organic process and enjoy the products, bread and beer. Up to this point in history, all bread was unfermented. Pounded or crushed grains were mixed with water and cooked into flatbreads, either on hot stones or in basic mud ovens. Given our ancestral knowledge of fruit fermentation, it is entirely plausible that brewing came before baking, and that yeast was then intentionally introduced to bread dough when a scoop of barm was carried from one corner of a Neolithic kitchen to another. Of course, the addition of yeast to bread dough may have been a purely serendipitous event. As with the discovery of, for example, penicillin and champagne, pure chance and human fallibility might have combined to change the world immeasurably for the better, by introducing us to leavened bread.

Yeasts are single-celled microscopic organisms, classified as fungi. With some 1,500 species identified to date, yeasts have great genetic diversity and they are everywhere: in the air, in the soil, on the skin of fruits and berries, on plant exudates and tree bark, on insects, on human skin, in the intestinal tracts of warm-blooded mammals, on seaweed, in fish and, more familiarly, in wine, beer and fermenting bread dough. Many species and their variants are highly localized. Numerous yeasts commonly associated with fermentation in bread have been isolated and identified, though it is believed that only a handful of them actually play a role in the leavening process. The two most important species in baking are *Candida humilis* and *Saccharomyces cerevisiae*.

The first person to actually see yeast cells was Dutch scientist Antonie van Leeuwenhoek, under an early microscope in the late seventeenth century, though he didn't even know what they were. Almost two centuries later, the great French chemist and founding father of microbiology, Louis Pasteur, finally proved, in 1857, that ethanol fermentation was caused by living microorganisms or yeasts. It is amazing to think that for at least five millennia, we baked leavened bread without understanding the first thing about yeasts. For all of that time, baking was a quotidian act of faith.

Pasteur's discovery, though hugely important, did not explain the full complexity of the fermentation process. During the 1930s, two German biochemists, Gustav Embden and Otto Meyerhof, revealed the sequence of reactions required to transform sugar to alcohol and carbon dioxide. More recently, microbiology has delved even further into the complex chain of continuous chemical and biological events that generate change in the ecological state of fermenting dough. We still don't understand every single part of the process, but we are getting there.

Generally, flour is metabolically in a resting state. Add water and that changes. Flour contains an enzyme, a biological catalyst consisting of protein, called amylase. This enzyme, which is activated on contact with water in the mixing bowl, starts to dine on starch that has been 'damaged' in the milling process, breaking tightly wound and tasteless balls of complex carbohydrates into sugars. As sugar levels rise, yeasts then release their own enzymes, notably one called zymase, which devour or metabolize the simple sugars. The yeasts respire aerobically at first, consuming oxygen in the dough. When the oxygen runs out, yeasts switch to anaerobic respiration and continue to process sugars, producing ethyl alcohol or ethanol (that emits a pungent smell, flavours the dough and eventually bakes off in the oven) and carbon dioxide (that makes the dough expand). One molecule of sugar is thus converted into two molecules of carbon dioxide and two molecules of alcohol. The simple and, to chemists, elegant equation for this is $C_6H_{12}O_6 \rightarrow 2C_2H_5OH + 2CO_2$.

Meanwhile, bacteria – generally, there are several species in dough, the majority of which belong to the genus *Lactobacillus*, the most common being *L. Sanfrancensis* – work in symbiosis with the fermenting yeasts, creating acetic acid, lactic acid and more alcohol. Lactic acid inscribes aromas into the dough and creates the sour taste in sourdough bread. It also contributes to the digestibility of bread, by breaking proteins down. Acetic acid acts as a preservative by lowering the pH, which prevents mould growth in the finished loaf. The yeasts also produce lysine, a basic amino acid and an essential nutrient in our diet. Lysine significantly improves the B-vitamin content of the dough. It also decreases the concentration of phytic acid, thereby making it easier for the human gut to digest starches, proteins and even some essential minerals like calcium.

You might reasonably expect the carbon dioxide gas produced by the feeding yeast to escape from the fermenting dough into the atmosphere. It does not. It is trapped, the consequence of a separate but contemporaneous chemical development in the dough that seals gas in. Gluten (the Latin word for 'glue') is formed in dough when its precursors called gliadin and glutenin – two proteins naturally present in wheat seeds and, to a lesser extent, other cereals like rye, to nourish the plant embryo during germination – combine when mixed with water to form a mesh. These two proteins contribute equally important properties that exist in productive tension. Gliadin gives dough 'extensibility', a baker's term that refers to the capacity of dough to stretch and hold air bubbles, without springing back to its former shape. Glutenin provides elasticity. In mixing or kneading dough, this mesh of gluten proteins re-arrange themselves and bond with others to form long chains of amino acids, creating a strong elastic network. This network captures the emitted gases, enabling the dough to stretch like a balloon, and thereby increase in volume or rise.

All of this will take place in a simple mixture of flour and water, if left for a long time. Add a substance already rich with yeasts and bacteria like sourdough starter, and the dough quickly becomes an intensively active, chemical laboratory. As a method of making grass seeds nourishing to humans, sourdough fermentation is an ingenious and ancient instance of food technology. The archaeological evidence is scant, but it seems that bakers in Egypt were beginning to master fermentation as early as the third millennium BC, though their loaves were not thoroughly aerated. They were probably more like muffins than modern sourdough loaves. The many bread fragments discovered in Egyptian tombs, including the exceptional three-cornered loaf in the British Museum that I had been to see, attest to this.

Over time, sailors and traders exported the secrets of dough management around the Mediterranean, to the Greek islands first, where keen rivalry existed between cities as to which produced the best bread, and then to Rome. The tomb of the baker Marcus Vergilius Eurysaces, an extant monument of almost royal magnificence near the Porta Maggiore in Rome, depicts in friezes all the elements of the baking process, including hand-kneading dough, which expedites the initial stages of fermentation. In the first century AD, the Romans began to perfect the art of fermentation, producing high-quality, risen loaves that we would recognize and relish eating. As John Cleese might have asked in Monty Python's *Life of Brian*: 'All right, but apart from the sanitation, the medicine, education, public order, irrigation, roads, the fresh water system, public health *and* delicious leavened bread, what have the Romans ever done for us?'

Mastering fermentation did not mean humans cast aside unleavened bread entirely, though. Flatbreads remain popular in many societies today. The chapatti in India is probably the best known, but there are numerous extant variations including *yufka*, which I had eaten with Tarık in Anatolia, *lavash* in Armenia and Iran, *piadina* from Romagna in Italy, *lepinja* in the Balkans, *tortilla* in North and Central America (made from finely ground maize flour), and Swedish *knäckebröd* (made from rye), to name a few. Unleavened breads remain easy and inexpensive to produce. In Europe, the poorer a region is, the better the chance of glimpsing the tail end of an ancient flatbread tradition. Of all the members of the flatbread family though, one stands out, because of its enduring symbolic value over millennia – matzah.

I ate matzah once, as a child. My parents were friends with a Jewish family who brought a box of it to our house. I was confused, firstly by the box, the style of which suggested it might contain something delicious like mint chocolates or Turkish delight, and then by the acclamation with which the adults ate these large, dry crackers. It looked nothing like bread, yet they bowed and curtsied with every bite. When I was allowed to try a piece, confusion turned to astonishment: it tasted like cardboard. For years, I had been wondering how matzah was made, and why it attracted such reverence.

'Look, look, see that? In ten seconds, the matzah is cooked. No, less than ten seconds. Eight seconds. It comes out of the oven, it cools, it's wrapped up and boxed. It's sent all over the world – all over the world! They make a tonne of matzah in this bakery every day – a tonne a day! Five days a week for seven months, which means, well – you do the maths. It's a lot of matzah,' Bentzion Roeber said, gesticulating wildly like an 'open outcry' commodities trader during a market crash, as he welcomed me to Kfar Chabad Bakery. Bentz, as he introduced himself, does not work at the bakery, but he had been co-opted to show me around because he speaks fluent English.

Matzah is an unleavened crispbread made from flour and water. It is eaten exclusively during the annual festival of Passover or Pesach, which commemorates the flight of the Israelites, an enslaved minority in pharaonic bondage, out of Egypt. In their urgent desire to be liberated, the Israelites left in a great hurry, following Moses to the Red Sea. As they departed, the Book of Exodus says, 'the people took their dough before it was leavened . . . And they baked unleavened cakes of the dough . . . it was not leavened because they were thrust out of Egypt and could not tarry.' In commemoration of this, the founding myth of Israel, and one which remains central to Jewish identity today, the faithful abstain from eating any leavened bread during the week-long festival. In its place, matzah is consumed with the symbolic weight of the millennia-old pursuit of salvation.

Kfar Chabad, near Tel Aviv, is the most famous 'handmade' matzah bakery in Israel. Established in 1950, it immediately set the highest rabbinical standards for matzah production and, through proselytizing about the importance of Passover, attracted dignitaries from all over the country, including prime ministers and presidents. The afternoon I arrived, the new American ambassador to Israel had just completed his tour.

'The Seder, the special meal on the first night of Pesach when families get together and talk about the Exodus, it's the most important meal of the year. Everybody wants the best matzah for this meal,' Bentz said. 'Everybody wants handmade matzah, everybody wants *shmurah* matzah. Let me show you how it's made.'

Shmurah, Bentz explained, is Hebrew for 'guarded'. The term refers to how the wheat and flour are processed and stored, following strict religious guidelines, to guarantee that no water comes into contact with the flour before it reaches the bakery. Inside the bakery, the principal focus of the process is to ensure the dough does not have time to rise, otherwise it is *chametz* or 'leavened bread' and invalidated for Passover according to Jewish law: it has to be thrown in the bin. Thus, there is a digital clock high on the wall, in the middle of the bakery, recording the time it takes to bake every batch of dough.

'Matzah has to be made in less than eighteen minutes.

That's what the rabbis say. When the next batch of flour comes into the bakery from the flour store, through this pipe here, then the clock starts . . . ready? Watch. Now!'

The flour came down a pipe and landed in a large metal mixing bowl. A man with thick glasses and a heavy grey beard broke into a trot with a mug of water that he poured over the flour. Another man with the forearms of a wrestler thrust his hands into the bowl and began clawing the water and flour together. The dough was then transferred to a work bench and kneaded noisily, by a team of men using metal rolling pins fixed at one end. Now in baguette-shape, each portion of dough was snipped with a cutter into a dozen discs that were distributed around a large metal table, like playing cards. A dozen more bearded men in matching blue bakery bibs and hairnets rolled the dough into thin, flat circles the size of dinner plates. Everybody was hopping up and down on the spot or jogging back and forth across the room, with jiggling ringlets out of synchrony. The cacophony was relentless. The whole scene was a form of choreographed chaos. It was like a Saturday night TV show – a hybrid of *The Generation Game* and *The Great British Bake Off*.

'Time, time. Look at the clock,' Bentz said, shaking my arm. He had toured the bakery many times, yet he was behaving like a kid who had just hit the jackpot on a fruit machine. Between each batch of dough, the bakers changed their bibs and washed their hands. Someone checked everyone's hands were dry. The tables were scrubbed down, to ensure no mote of the previous batch was left behind. Bentz and I strode around the corner into a pulsing blanket of heat. The wafer-thin circles of dough were being flopped over long wooden poles wrapped in brown paper and thrust into two brick-vaulted ovens that glowed orange. Seconds later, the crisp rounds of speckled matzah were extracted and stacked in a pile on a wooden cart.

'Twelve minutes,' Bentz said, throwing his palms up, as if offering a benediction. 'Now you need to try some. You don't have to wait for the Seder supper, my friend.'

Bentz took a broken fragment of warm matzah, snapped it in two and handed me a piece. I knew what it would taste like.

'Delicious, huh? Of course it is. It's the "food of faith",' Bentz said. I nodded out of propriety. He smiled beatifically and clapped me on the shoulder. His work was done. Waiting for my bus back to Jerusalem, I thought of an essay I had read about the symbolism of matzah. It is flat and plain, like the meek person who comes to God without pretence, reminding people to be appreciative and humble at Passover. Leavened bread, on the other hand, is puffed up with pride. Matzah also represents the misery of slavery: it is the 'bread of affliction' (Deuteronomy 16:3). At the same time, it symbolizes freedom.

Bread is a primary theme not just for the Jewish faith, but throughout the Christian Bible, from Genesis to Revelation. Jesus was born in Bethlehem — *beth-lehem* is Hebrew for 'house of bread'. The Evangelists who portrayed the life and teachings of Christ in the New Testament Gospels, written between 50 and 100 AD, seem particularly concerned with bread, and the whole agricultural cycle that provided it. Many parables relate to ploughing, sowing, harvesting and baking. In the 'Feeding of the Five Thousand' miracle, Jesus satisfies the hunger of a large crowd of followers with five loaves and two fishes, making the point that bread is everywhere, and is everyone's: if you break it and share it, it keeps giving. The title 'Bread of Life' is given to Jesus by the author of the Gospel of St John, following the feeding of the multitude.

Jesus and his disciples wished to establish an earthly nation of plenty, a realm of bread, where replete people could transcend the spiritual kingdom to be nourished by the bread of God. When Jesus teaches the disciples the Lord's Prayer, he asks foremost: 'Give us this day our daily bread.' Hunger was, very likely, a widespread issue in the Holy Land during biblical times. Judea was an imperial territory under Roman rule. A large part of the barley and wheat harvest was collected annually in the form of a grain toll and sent to Rome. There must have been local bread shortages.

Paramount among biblical bread references is the Last Supper, the fraternal meal Jesus shared with his Apostles before he was crucified. According to the version of events in the Gospel of St Matthew, 'as they were eating, Jesus took bread and blessed it and broke it, and gave it to his disciples and said, "Take, eat: this is my body".' With these words, Christianity in effect co-opted bread as a principal religious symbol, and one we have been arguing about ever since. Some Christian denominations maintain that the Last Supper was the traditional Seder meal, celebrating Passover. In which case, the bread Jesus held up, gave thanks for, broke and distributed to his disciples to eat, thus initiating the first part of the Christian celebration of Holy Communion, the greatest of the sacraments and the central act of church life, was matzah. Jews were required to eat it at Pesach even then. If it was matzah, theologians have observed that it symbolizes the suitability of Jesus for sacrifice: he is not leavened with sin. If, on the other hand, it was risen bread, then it is symbolic of the Resurrection and Ascension of Christ.

Following the Last Supper, Holy Communion bread was leavened for the next thousand years. In the eleventh century, communion bread was one of the earthly factors, and a major point of friction, in a larger theological and political row between Pope Leo IX in Rome and Michael Cerularius, the Patriarch of Constantinople. That row led to the Great Schism of 1054, one of the most significant events in the history of Christianity. To this day, members of the Roman Catholic Church (together with Armenian and Maronite Christians) celebrate communion with unleavened bread. The 200 million or so adherents of the Eastern Orthodox Church receive the Eucharistic Host in the form of leavened bread. The ecumenical dialogues are still raging.

Away from religion, bread has been an essential cultural symbol that humans have turned to again and again, to celebrate familial occasions and ancestral dates in the calendar. There are Winter Solstice breads in Germany, New Year breads prepared by young women in central Europe representing purification and renewal, *Iftar* breads eaten by Muslims to break the daily fast during Ramadan, and breads baked as part of engagement ceremonies in India. In medieval Poland, bagels were given to women after childbirth. On All Souls'

Day in Mexico, *pan de muertos* or 'bread of the dead' is offered to the deceased. From the multitude of symbolic breads that we have devised to help make sense of human existence over the last eight or nine thousand years, however, one stands out for the breadth of its cultural resonance: wedding bread.

The wedding loaf, symbolizing fertility and prosperity, has roots in prehistory and myth. It certainly seems to have been an established custom within the Persian Empire by the fourth century BC. When Alexander the Great married the princess Roxana, reputed to be the most beautiful woman in the world, on the summit of the sky-fortress Sisimithres, in Central Asia, in 327 BC, there was a great wedding banquet. Before the guests, Alexander and his teenage bride cut a loaf of bread with a sword and ate half each. The tradition passed directly to the Romans, for whom the most solemn form of marriage was made binding when the bride and groom sacramentally cut a loaf made of emmer flour, offered the largest part to the gods and ate the rest, thereby breaking bread together as a couple for the first time. This ancient custom has survived into the modern era in many western cultures, in the form of the wedding cake.

The humble peasant tradition of the wedding bread or loaf, which survived in Britain until the late Middle Ages, still lingers, notably in the Slavic regions of central and eastern Europe, and across the Near East. The main features of this wedding bread – a round, braided loaf made from wheat flour embellished with symbols – are highly consistent across Poland, Russia, Ukraine, Belarus and Bulgaria. In Ukraine, the wedding bread or *korovai* symbolizes, among other things, the whole community's blessings for the couple. According to tradition in Russia, *karavai* is made on the Saturday night before the wedding, expressly by women who are content with their family lives and have children. They knead their experiences of domestic happiness, their fertility, the fate of their own marriages, and even their dreams into the dough.

Last year, our neighbours, who have spent time in Poland, asked my wife to bake a loaf for a ceremony to renew their vows, after ten years of marriage. The loaf was slightly out of its cultural context, in a barn in the Black Mountains of Wales, but it was unquestionably an honour to be asked to bake it. As my wife trialled different loaves and the ceremony approached, we both felt the weight of the ancient tradition pressing up against the ticking clock in our diminutive kitchen.

The immemorial convention of wedding bread extends beyond the Slavic world into Armenia, where a piece of *lavash* is placed on the bride's shoulder. In Romania, godparents of the bride and groom break a sweet, brioche-style loaf called *turta miresei* over the bride's head. Similarly, in central Greece, the wedding bread called *provenda*, the aroma of which is said to symbolize the sweetness of marriage, is broken by the bride over her own head. In the Republic of North Macedonia, named after the region where Alexander the Great was born, the godfather of the bride dances with a special, sweetened bread called *koluk*. Perhaps the best-known ceremonial bread, and a pillar of Jewish cuisine in many parts of the world today, is challah. At Jewish wedding ceremonies, a rabbi or family elder gives a blessing over the challah, before it is broken. New life, and the party, may then begin.

'Challah is not just for weddings. No. Everybody has challah for Shabbat, everyone, every week, in every Jewish home, everywhere in the world,' Iris Saraf-Reinharts said, wagging a finger at me. 'Orthodox Jews, they buy ten. Non-orthodox, they buy one. Normally I bake my own at home, but today I don't have time so I buy one of these Lendner challahs. Don't they look so good?'

Iris is a cook and culinary tour guide in Jerusalem. The daughter of Ashkenazi Jews who emigrated from Poland in the late twentieth century, she had agreed to show me round a few bakeries. We had connected through friends in the global real-bread network that I was beginning to weave my way into. She is dark-haired, handsome, over-brimming with humanity, and maternal. Watching her sashay through the grimy backstreets of Jerusalem made me think of Ida Arnold, the unlikely heroine in Graham Greene's novel *Brighton Rock*.

Lendner Bakery, a dimly lit stone cavern on a backstreet in the neighbourhood of Beit Yisrael, has been in the same family for 130 years. Before the Lendners emmigrated to Israel, they were bakers in the city of Czernowitz, in Romania (now part of Ukraine), for generations. Today, the Lendner bakery only opens on Thursdays and Fridays, and only produces challah for the Sabbath, Judaism's day of rest.

'For many people in Jerusalem, Shabbat is just not Shabbat without a Lendner challah. They bake around 2,000 in these two huge brick ovens, and they sell out every week,' Iris said, handing me a braided loaf the size of a rugby ball, with a shiny umber and auburn crust sprinkled generously with sesame seeds.

The traditional ingredients of challah are white flour, water, salt, sugar, yeast and eggs. After the dough has risen for the first time, it is rolled into rope-shaped pieces that are then woven together. These braided threads are said to symbolize the chain of life, while the loaf itself symbolizes 'manna', the food that God provided for the Israelites during their years wandering in the desert. The finished shape also faintly echoes an ear of wheat. Many cultures enjoy braided, egg-enriched breads but challah is first among them, in its spiritual and ceremonial significance. The word 'challah' is biblical in origin. It refers to the commandment in the Torah (the law of God as recorded in the first five books of the Hebrew scriptures) to set aside a portion of dough as an offering to God. The term was first applied to bread in the Middle Ages, probably in southern Germany.

'There are special three-metre-long wedding challahs, chal-lahs for Jewish holidays and challahs for the firstborn son, but week in, week out, the smell of freshly baked challah on Thursday night is the smell of Shabbat,' Iris said, tearing a piece from the loaf to reveal the soft, fluffy off-white crumb.

'Think about all the ethnic groups in Jerusalem – Iraqis, Persians, Poles, Germans, Romanians, Russians, Hungarians, Yemenis, Kurds, and then . . . Ethiopians, Azeris, Uzbeks, Tatars, Moldovans, Armenians, Belarusians and more. Each community has its own habits. Each community has its own breads and they are all so proud of their breads. But the one thing all communities have in common is challah, because it is in the Bible. Challah defines us. We bless challah before eating it. It tastes so good too.'

Emerging from the bakery, we walked through the sunlit streets of Mea Sharim, the ultra-Orthodox neighbourhood of Jerusalem. Piles of rubbish were waiting to be collected under blossoming trees. The ritual of Bi'ur Chametz, literally 'cleaning out the leaven', is an important part of domestic preparations for Passover, Iris explained, particularly among communities who observe the scriptures strictly. Families empty out food cupboards and fridges in an exhaustive spring clean, before ceremoniously collecting the last crumbs of leavened products with spoons and even feathers. Many then cleanse their kitchen utensils and set fire to the last of the leavened bread. I thought of trying to clean my own kitchen in the same fashion. Over years of baking sourdough bread, starter has managed to get into every nook and crevice.

Our next stop was Nechama's Bakery, in the Bukharan neighbourhood. Sweating bakers were preparing *nan-e barbari*, a leavened flatbread popular in Iran, around a glowing oven. Iris pointed out Yazdi breads from central Iran, pretzels, deep-fried Hungarian *lángos* and *ka'ak*, popular Palestinian bagels covered in sesame seeds, as well as a huge choice of pastries and cookies. There was also a range of Yemeni breads that I had never seen before, including *lahoh* (a spongy, pancake-type bread), *malawah* (a sweet, flaky breakfast pancake), *kubaneh* (a yeasted dough rolled in layers and baked slowly overnight) and *khaliat nahal* (a cheese-filled honeycomb bread dripping with orange blossom syrup).

A mile away, in Machane Yehuda market, the pre-Shabbat shopping frenzy was in full cry when we arrived at midday. There were extravagantly bearded old men in black, belted overcoats and hats with ribbon trim, teenage girls with acne in army fatigues carrying assault rifles, glamorous women in silk shirts and designer sunglasses, dreadlocked travellers with tattooed calves, and old ladies with bloated feet bulging out of pink sliders pulling tartan shopping trolleys. Known locally as the 'Shuk', Machane Yehuda has been the underbelly of Jerusalem since it was established during the Ottoman period, over a century ago. Originally an open-air bazaar for Arab merchants selling local produce, it has developed into one of the world's great covered food markets. Iris and I tasted pomegranate tea, *burekas, baklava,* exquisite hummus, olive oil, goats' cheeses, dried mulberries, chocolate pastries, halva and tahini, as we hustled and snaked through the stalls. Twenty years ago, campaigning Israeli politicians came here to be photographed with the *amcha,* the hard-working, leather-handed masses. In the past decade, though, gentrification has seen a vibrant dining scene emerge out of the Holy City's tapestry of Middle Eastern, North African, Mediterranean and Eastern European cuisines – a trend I had come to Jerusalem to write about for a magazine at home.

Bread has been part of that transformation. The sweet smell of baked loaves was everywhere in the market, despite the competition from freshly ground coffee, hot pastries, fish, spices and cheese. The bread stalls in the market are supplied by bakeries in the surrounding streets. Trays of hot loaves were constantly being ferried above the swell of shoppers.

Traditional golden challahs were piled high, but Iris also pointed out wholemeal challahs, maize challahs, challahs with raisins and challahs baked with smoked paprika, thyme and black pepper. The newest wave of bakeries in the Shuk, including Teller and Russell's, are disciples of sourdough. Their artisanal bread wares could have been for sale on market carts in Shoreditch, Brooklyn, Berlin or Seattle. There were brick-shaped Russian rye breads, sourdough *boules*, focaccias, olive oil and rosemary *épis* shaped like wheat ears, German multigrain breads baked with rolled oats and flax seeds, wholemeal baguettes and bagels.

At 3 p.m. the wave of shoppers parted, as if the whistle had gone in a game of medieval mob football. Shabbat had begun. The hawkers stopped hawking. Young lads started to clean up. Stall owners set out chairs and lit cigars. There was a waft of marijuana smoke. The last of the bread loaves were carried back to the bakeries, to be sold at half price to waiting queues. When Iris went home to cook Shabbat supper, I walked down Jaffa Street to Damascus Gate ('Bab al-Amud' in Arabic), the largest of the Old City's seven gates and the main entrance to the Muslim Quarter. Just inside the gate, at the top of Al-Wad Road, on the corner of a market plaza teeming with pilgrims, tourists, street traders, shoppers and beggars, I met Iris's friend, Adem. He was a short, wiry Palestinian in a singlet, with deep-set green eyes, an electric smile and the upper body of a bantamweight boxer. The tapestry of flour and dried dough on his bare arms and cheeks told me I had got the right man. Inside the bakery, Adem and his colleagues were producing a continuous supply of 'Ka'ak Al Quds', or 'Jerusalem bagels', mini pittas and *mannakish*, an Arabic leavened flatbread akin to pizza and Indian naan, which I had come to see them bake.

The dough, made of flour, water, salt and dried yeast, was mixed in a large metal vat with an electric dough hook. Adem then scooped it out by hand, nimbly moulding each hunk in the air and placing them in neat rows on a wooden tray covered in bran. The trays were then stacked in a corner. When the dough had risen a little, Adem lifted each saucer out and, with great dexterity, flipped them from hand to hand to create a dinner plate-sized round of thinner dough. With his knuckles, he pressed down repeatedly on the dough, sculpting rows of small indentations – the word *mannakish* probably derives from a medieval Arabic word for decorative designs. Favourite toppings for *mannakish* include minced lamb, cheeses and spinach. Adem, however, was coating his rounds of dimpled dough with za'atar, the aromatic, bitter blend of salt, sumac, thyme, oregano and toasted sesame seeds, all soaked in olive oil. He ladled the za'atar on to the rounds and slid the tray into the conveyor-belt oven. Two minutes later, the baked breads, slightly puffed up with crispy, brown spots around the edge and glistening with bubbling oil in the centre, dropped on to a board. Basil, Adem's colleague, gathered a dozen on a tray and carried them out through the open doorway into the blazing sunlight, to the street stall on the plaza. A few minutes after that, they were being consumed by pilgrims making their way to the Via Dolorosa.

Adem understood more English than he spoke. I explained that I had tried and failed to make good *mannakish za'atar*.

Where was I going wrong? Was it the oven temperature? Or my homemade za'atar? Perhaps it was the way I handled and knuckled the dough? Adem shrugged. He pressed three folded breads wrapped in newspaper under my arm and looked insulted when I proffered a twenty-shekel note. Basil was calling him. He hung a sinewy arm round my shoulder and searched my face with his dark green eyes: 'No man can bake every bread,' he said. Then he turned and hurried back into the sweltering darkness.

Watching Nicolas Supiot knead dough in a wooden trough or *pétrin*, as he called it, on a two-day heritage grain workshop beside the sea in West Wales, I realized Adem was right. Since planting my wheat, I had been experimenting with a madcap variety of breads from around the world. I had tried making *lavash*, focaccia, *fougasse, nan-e barbari*, beetroot sourdough, Georgian *puri*, a Swedish rye bread called *limpa*, seeded multigrain bread, potato rosemary bread, Welsh seaweed sourdough and more. Travelling across continents to antique lands through bread, without leaving my own kitchen, had been a pleasure. But, as I was about to start baking with my own flour, I needed to engage with the timeless baker's challenge of evoking the fullest potential from my wheat. To this end, I had to focus – on doing one thing, and doing it well.

I decided to concentrate on baking a simple, country sourdough loaf, or *pain au levain* in French. The elemental ingredients are sourdough starter, flour, water and salt. Plus a bit of human sweat. First, I would bake with emmer and Hen Gymro separately. I already knew that working with wholemeal flour would be tricky, compared to baking with 'strong white bread flour', which is made from hard wheat and has a high protein content. Strong white flour leavens dough readily and produces large, upstanding, porous loaves. I would then try mixing the two wholemeal flours. And if I could not get my wholemeal dough to rise, I would add a measure of organic white flour from a local mill. Anne's prediction – that I would be baking pancakes for a while – was already haunting my dreams.

Nicolas Supiot has been growing, harvesting, threshing, milling and baking with organic landrace wheat populations for twenty years, in his native Brittany. Through his commitment to understanding every part of the bread-making process – from how the microorganisms in the soil influence taste to the organic matter and minerals in the salt that is added to dough – he has become a mentor to the burgeoning ordination of new *paysans boulangers* or 'peasant farmer-bakers' in Europe. Nicolas even has a manifesto of agricultural and bread-making values, which states: 'We consider bread and agricultural products as spiritual nourishment and physically vital as well as emotionally, culturally and spiritually healing.' Part material object, part symbol of respect for nature, his bread occupies the crossroads between the temporal and the sacred. If the history of modern bread, which begins with milling flour in steel roller mills, can be told as a series of steps removing the fundamental elements of the process – the uncertainty, the sanctity, the comparative slowness of the biological activity, the nutritional value of the seeds and the flavour – Nicolas Supiot is striving to reinstate them all.

Stocky, with tanned skin and heavy eyebrows, and dressed in thick, brown corduroy trousers, a collarless shirt and a trilby, Nicolas looked more like an Edwardian gamekeeper than a bread guru. He scooped enough flour for twenty or so large loaves into the trough and 'woke it up', in his words, with his hands. 'It is vital to bring spirit to what we do. It makes our work pleasurable,' he said. In many cultures, bread making remains an act of devotion. In Armenia, I had read, women whisper dreams and blessings into the dough, in the belief that it has a memory: when the bread is eaten, those blessings are realized. It is an appealing thought, that dough might somehow absorb the energy and emotions of the person who kneads it, and pass them on.

When the humidity in the flour was right, Nicolas said a brief prayer. Then he added water and the roomful of eager acolytes fell silent. His forearms swished and swirled through the emulsion, as if he was performing an ancient, reverential hand dance. He was firm but tender. From time to time, more flour was added at the ends of the trough. Nothing was measured. In fact, Nicolas preaches the development of intuition and flexibility in baking, rather than perfecting small technicalities within the process. Recipes change, he said, according to variable factors like temperature, the variety of wheat, how long ago the flour was milled and even the seasons. Fermentation time for the same dough in winter could be fifteen hours, and in summer, five hours.

Sweating heavily and breathing hard, Nicolas worked in silence. He vigorously hauled dough from the ends of the trough to the middle with a scraper, like a spaniel digging up a mole hill. I was reminded that in France, the baker's boy who did the kneading used to be called *le geindre*, or 'the groaner'. Scrape, stretch, slap, clump, thump, huff and puff – kneading dough sounded like a *soigneur* at work, taking knots of muscle out of a cyclist's thighs, after a gruelling mountain stage of the Tour de France. When Nicolas began to get really carried away with the stretching and folding, the noise reminded me of men wrestling. I thought of Oliver Reed and Alan Bates grappling in front of the fire, in the film version of D. H. Lawrence's *Women in Love*. The dough sucked and surged back and forth until it was smooth, with the structure of setting jelly.

Nicolas gently tamped the surface down into the trough with open palms, as you might pat a baby's bottom dry. With a final flourish of his hands, the service was over. Nicolas went off to mop himself clean. The dough would be left to ferment for ten or more hours. The congregation of people drifted outside into the sea-salted sunlight. I felt like I had witnessed a religious ceremony. Clearly, I needed to re-evaluate my relationship with bread. The bar had just been raised.

The alternative to using the time-honoured method of fermenting dough with a natural leavening agent like sourdough starter is manufactured yeast. The Fleischmann brothers established the first yeast factory in Cincinnati, Ohio, in 1868. By the 1880s, they were mass-producing a purified monoculture of the naturally occurring yeast species, *Saccharomyces cerevisiae*, literally 'sweet fungus of beer'. This new form of commercial yeast was raised on a diet of molasses, then diluted, washed, filtered, dried and cooled before being powdered or compressed into cakes. There were other yeast manufacturers, but the Fleischmann brothers, ambitious immigrants from Hungary, stole a yard on their competitors. By 1900, Fleischmann's was the world's leading yeast brand and a household name in the USA.

Manufactured yeast, which coincided with the advent of steel roller mills and the availability of cheap white flour, immediately appealed to large-scale bakeries. At the time, the majority of bakeries in Europe were still getting yeast from breweries, but a major change in the brewing industry in the 1880s jeopardized that supply. Commercial yeast replaced it. Rather than rely on a complex community of unknown, unseen fungi and bacteria to leaven bread, here was a single species of yeast optimized for the job. It was measured, linear, predictable and reliable. Fundamentally, as dough made with this new style of yeast took less time to rise, operating costs fell.

Unfortunately for the consumer, speed and control came at a price. Real bread made from slowly leavened dough has textural properties, structure, keeping qualities and complex layers of flavour that bread made from speedily fermented dough mixed with a yeast monoculture cannot replicate. Slow-fermented bread also affords an array of nutritional benefits: it reduces the rate at which we absorb carbohydrates (put another way, it has a lower glycaemic index); it changes rapidly digested sugars into non-digestible fibres called 'prebiotics' that pass through the stomach and into the colon, where they feed the biota that live within us; nutrients present in wheat like iron, zinc and magnesium, as well as several B vitamins, become easier for our bodies to absorb; finally, there is a corpus of research that suggests lengthy fermentation makes gluten proteins more digestible to some people.

Kneading dough, which kick-starts the fermentation process, is where the intrigue in baking begins for me: it is the soul of bread making. Having observed Nicolas Supiot, I was keen to have a go with my own flour. Once I had mixed my first measure of emmer with water, starter and salt, I turned it out of the bowl on to a lightly oiled, slate worktop in the kitchen. It looked like something you might remove from the bottom of a cement mixer. The uneven pile of grout had hills, ridges, cirques and truncated summits. I took a handful. I tried to lift and fold it, as I would do normally, kneading dough made with strong white bread flour. The clump came free in my hand. I tried to scrape it off my hand. It got stuck to the scraper. Then it was all over my other hand. It was like working with mortar. Just stickier. I added more flour. That made things worse. I tried to lift and fold again. Dough got stuck to my arms. By this stage, it was all over my apron and on my shoes. There was dough in the sink and on the taps. There were even florets of dough in my hair. My wife walked into the kitchen.

'I need help,' I said.

'Are you trying to re-create the Sellotape scene from *Paddington Bear*, but with bread dough?' she said, and walked out.

I thought of Nicolas Supiot's Zen-like state, up to his elbows in the wooden trough, and I resisted firing off offensive oaths. I also thought of Edward Espe Brown, the author of *The*

Tassajara Bread Book, who wrote: 'When you knead bread, you're kneading all the channels and acupuncture points in your hands. Whether you call that a spiritual benefit or a physiological one, doing something with your hands is just incredibly invigorating to your whole body.' This was about as invigorating as searching for a wedding ring in a municipal sewer.

Normally, I love kneading dough. I love how the initial gummy texture diminishes with each lift and fold; how the inert paste of flour and water re-forms into a smooth, shapely bolus with suppleness and body. By degrees, the dough becomes more silky, elastic and tenacious, as the gluten network forms like sinews firming up in a tensing muscle. But this was nothing like that. I had read that wheat varieties like emmer struggle to establish gluten networks, and that the dough requires the baker's complete attention. Still, I had not expected it to be quite so tricky. I may have added too much water. Maybe I needed more salt: salt not only adds flavour to bread, it also tightens the gluten network in dough. Perhaps I should have left the dough to rest before kneading. Certainly, I had failed to adequately delegate powers and responsibilities to the tens of millions of microbes in the dough. I had much to learn about baking bread with wholemeal, stoneground flour. After twenty minutes, dough was spread even further – all over the floor, on my clothes and on the dog, who was padding it round the kitchen – but it was, finally, beginning to cohere. Emotionally exhausted, I scraped it back into the mixing bowl and went into the garden for a hose down.

Twelve hours later, at the end of the first or 'bulk'

fermentation on winter timings in our chilly kitchen, the dough had risen, a little. It had not doubled in size, as I had hoped. There was a yeasty aroma, with a hint of alcohol and vinegar. I scraped the dough on to a floured worktop. It had no body. It was still sticky. I folded and shaped it as well as I could, with floured hands and a delicate touch. Flouring my hands again, I placed the dough in a bamboo basket or 'banneton', for the final prove, or *apprêt* in French, before baking. By this point in the process, the dough is supposed to be relaxed, elastic and smooth, like human skin. During the final prove it should rise again, to reach the peak of its exultation moments before going into the oven. I recalled Michael Pollan, who wrote in *Cooked: A Natural History of Transformation*: 'not one of the bakers I had read or talked to had adequately prepared me for the erotics of leavened, shaped dough.' And Pollan is not alone in this sentiment. Other, generally male writers have noted how sensuous dough is. Not for me, at least not this time. My carcass of dough had all the eroticism of cold sick. And who wants to bake that?

CHAPTER 6

Le Pain Se Lève: Baking

'Arise, and eat bread, and let thine heart be merry.'

1 Kings 21:7

'I'm not being funny or anything, but what is that?' Kitty, my teenage daughter, said, as I pulled a loaf from the oven. I ignored her. I put the loaf on a cooling rack in a corner of the kitchen as Lucas, my teenage son walked in.

'Ah, excellent,' he said. 'Is this one a weapon, to brick a burglar to death? Or just another Stone Age frisbee?' Though it was getting harder, I ignored him too.

Baking with my own flour was not going well. The bread was edible, but this loaf, like all the others, was far from the ideal of a beautiful, crisp, round, risen *boule*; an ideal that I had conceived long ago and nursed through months spent sowing, harvesting, threshing and milling. The word 'loaf' derives from the Old English 'hlaf', which may have Germanic roots, but possibly derives from another Old English word, 'hlifian', for 'to raise higher, to tower'. The loaf on the cooling rack was 30cm by 20cm, oval-shaped, irregular in form and, as my children were intimating, flat. It was 3cm at the highest point. There was no hint of 'hlifian'. It looked like a vintage leather rugby ball that had been deflated and soaked in a water trough for a year, trampled by bullocks and then left to dry in the Danakil Depression. It had all the loft and eminence of a hardened cow-pat. The cold truth was – every loaf I had baked with my own wholemeal flour had been a flop. And the Llanthony & Valley District Show was edging closer.

Entering a loaf into the baking class of the fiercely contested produce competitions at our local agricultural show in the heart of the Black Mountains was my wife's idea: 'You need a focus,' she said. 'You need to work out what is going wrong. It's a technical problem, but you need to work out how to fix it, and fast. The Romans baked better bread than you.'

Correction. The Romans baked better *wholemeal* bread than me. I had mastered baking sourdough bread with strong white bread flour long ago. White flour is a standardized commodity that behaves in predictable ways. Once you have the knack, it is easy to bake with. My best white sourdough *boules* looked like the loaves on the covers of baking books. Some of them even met my wife's high standards. Making bread with stone-ground wholemeal flour made from heritage wheat is different, though. The flour is biologically complex and unpredictable. The process is more demanding and nuanced. The margin for error is reduced. Everything from the enzyme activity in the starter and the style of kneading, to the proving time and the temperature of the oven has to be spot on. In short, baking with stoneground wholemeal flour is much harder.

The main issue is the bran. The tiny scales and flakes of bran produced by the force of the millstones are hard and sharp-edged. They act like knives in fermenting dough, slicing through the chains of gluten as quickly as they form, preventing the dough from trapping gases and rising. Exasperated by my lack of progress, I rang Andy Forbes. He had provided sound advice when I planted, harvested and threshed my wheat. As well as being an expert on heritage varieties, he is also a skilled baker: 'Hmmm,' he said. 'Common problem. Try a procedure called *autolyse*.'

I had to look it up: it is a French word for a simple, additional step in the baking process whereby you pre-mix flour and water, then leave it to rest for an hour or more before adding starter and salt. The technique was introduced – or quite possibly re-introduced, as it might have been employed traditionally and forgotten – by Professor Raymond Calvel, the French chemist, author and baker, and one of the men credited with putting artistry back into French baking in the late twentieth century. Calvel's procedure offers several advantages: kneading time is reduced; the resulting dough is generally easier to work and shape; and, because the natural carotenoids in flour take less of a pounding, the bread tends to have deeper, more complex flavours, aromas and colour. As flour absorbs water slowly during the *autolyse*, not only does the bran soften (reducing its destructive effect on the chains of gluten), but also the development of an elastic network begins before the dough is handled.

Reading about *autolyse* on a variety of nerdy websites for sourdough junkies, I realized that adopting the technique might be the key to making my bread rise. At the same time, I decided to refine other aspects of my baking process. I changed the feeding regimen for my starters; I revised the time between primary and secondary fermentation; finally,

I decided to build my own wood-fired 'Pompeii' bread oven, in the hope (rather than the expectation) that the effort and cost would magically transform my loaves in time for the Show.

When Mount Vesuvius erupted in 79 AD, a cloud of volcanic ash fell upon the city of Pompeii, encasing the minutiae of daily life as it ebbed and flowed. The wealth of archaeological finds unearthed 1,700 years later included the remains of some thirty operational bakeries, with bread ovens attached. In one oven, eighty-one carbonized loaves were found, buried as they baked, many shaped like petalled flowers and still bearing the baker's stamp. The ovens discovered in Pompeii vary in size and degree of dilapidation, but they are all round, similarly vaulted with flues to vent off smoke, and constructed with bricks and doors that could be sealed. This suggests great homogeneity in design and building standards in Roman

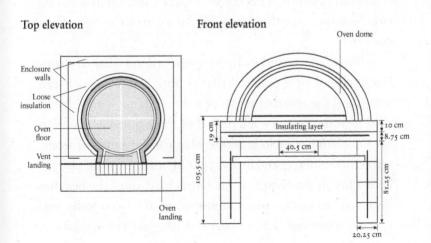

Top elevation

Enclosure walls
Loose insulation
Oven floor
Vent landing
Oven landing

Front elevation

Oven dome
Insulating layer
10 cm
8.75 cm
40.5 cm
19 cm
105.5 cm
81.25 cm
20.25 cm

times. Remarkably, those same design and building standards are effectively extant today. When I searched the internet for a DIY bread-oven blueprint, I kept coming across plans that replicated the ovens in Pompeii. When I spoke to my neighbour, Ben, who has an oven in his garden, he said: 'You definitely want a Pompeii-style oven. You can build one in a long weekend. Actually, with your DIY skills, give it a month.'

There are bakers who swear by the distinct qualities that wood-fired ovens infuse into bread. These qualities do not come from the wood. Rather, they come both from the steam that builds up inside an oven containing a full batch of loaves, as water in the dough vaporizes, and from the way heat is stored and then released from the hearth and walls. Steam helps the crust remain moist and pliable, allowing each loaf to rise to its maximum height, before the crust hardens. Furthermore, as the dough is only placed inside the oven after the wood-fire has been removed, bread bakes as the temperature drops. This critical aspect – baking in a 'falling oven' – is not something I could achieve in our ancient range cooker.

A bread oven traditionally comprises a dome-shaped chamber enclosed by a material that is both refractory – it can withstand the thermal shock of a direct flame – and able to hold heat for an extended period of time. Suitable materials for the chamber include adobe, clay, certain kinds of stone, refractory concrete and many types of brick. In principle, you light a fire in the chamber that burns hard, until the heat has removed the black carbon deposited on the oven walls, and they are white hot. The embers and ashes are then raked out.

Heat radiates from every surface. When the temperature of the oven is right, you are ready to bake. The dough is placed on the oven hearth or 'sole' and the door is shut tight.

As it transpired, my wholemeal bread came good before the wood-fired oven was finished. Through integrating the *autolyse* procedure, and honing my fermentation schedule, my dough began to rise – with vim. I bought new bannetons and started baking in an old, cast-iron casserole dish that Mum handed down years ago. I began baking every day, distributing my experimental loaves to neighbours, like alms. At times, it felt like I was setting up a micro-bakery. I could certainly feel the intensification of the labour in my back, from bending over to knead and stooping to put loaves in the oven. I had, however, managed to avoid the other ailments, like 'baker's asthma' (from inhaling flour) and 'baker's eczema' (when flour particles and yeast spores get under the skin), which have plagued commercial bakers throughout history.

One morning in spring, as the birds in the wood beyond the house were lustily heralding the day, I opened the oven door, pulled out the casserole dish and flipped the loaf on to a cooling rack. There it was: a perfectly risen round loaf with a dark crust – made from wheat that I had grown. It was as good as ideal. The hue and shape of it, which alone can inspire a rudimentary form of hunger, were excellent. The crust was quivering with electric charge. The 'ears' of crust, where the dough had ripped open, were upturned and proud, like slanted rock faults on a beach formed by the collision of tectonic plates. I bent over to listen to the pianissimo crackling sounds and whispers, called 'singing' and beloved of craft bakers, which the blistered crust made as it began to cool and shrink. Holding the loaf in a tea towel, I tapped the bottom with a finger. The hollow timbre, like the sound of a distant bass drum, assured me that all the moisture had dissipated – another clue that prefigures good flavour.

I had finally produced a stoneground wholemeal loaf that I was happy to put my stamp on. In fact, it looked like a loaf that might have come out of the Poilâne bakery in Paris. I walked round the table admiring it, though my feet hardly touched the ground, such was my sense of elation. Then I photographed it with my phone. Straight away, I saved the image as my lock screen. I just had to pray my children never found out.

The most famous baking dynasty of modern times was established in 1932, when the 23-year-old Pierre Poilâne migrated from a small farm in Normandy to the Left Bank of the Seine in Paris, with a recipe for an Arcadian loaf in his head. On renting the property at 8 rue du Cherche-Midi – the site of a bakery since the French Revolution – Pierre's first act was to replace the basement oven. Maison Poilâne now has a large baking facility outside Paris with twenty-four village bakery-style ovens, each with its own team of bakers. *Pains Poilâne* are exported around the world to over forty countries and the company grosses ten million pounds annually. At the heart of the Poilâne brand is their signature loaf, a two-kilo, naturally fermented, mahogany-brown, flour-coated, thick-crusted sourdough loaf called a *miche*, famously baked in a wood-fired oven. Some 5,000 are sold every day. At least one is delivered to the Élysée Palace, the residence of the French president. The actors Isabelle Adjani and Gérard Depardieu are fans, as were Frank Sinatra and Lauren Bacall. For many craft bakers today, the Poilâne *miche* is a reference point for excellence. The American baker and author Peter Reinhart wrote that the loaf is an 'icon of the bread revolution'. In my second-hand copy of his book *The Bread Baker's Apprentice*, the pages devoted to the 'Poilâne-style *miche*' are covered in flecks of starter and fingerprints of coagulated flour – a form of ornamentation attesting to the previous owner's reverence for the recipe.

Lionel Poilâne, son of Pierre, took over the business in 1973. Using what he described as 'retro-innovation', he adapted ancient baking practices to create dense, dark peasant loaves for a new generation of bread eaters. He preached 'time and repetition' as the pathway to baking great bread. Still, recipes are not written down, ingredients are never weighed and the temperature of the ovens is judged from experience. Poilâne bakers have to learn by feel: they have to develop the 'baker's touch'. Lionel famously said: 'One only makes good bread if one truly loves bread.' Lionel had more than love, though; he also possessed a flair for business and panache for publicity. He once baked a whole bedroom of bread for Salvador Dalí, and edible masks for the French sculptor César. With his wife, Lionel created what was then an anomaly – a successful baking business producing artisanal bread, at scale. He was also an influential early leader in the conscious movement to save French bread.

Bread needed saving in the 1970s, even in France, where bread culture had been strong for centuries. As the historian

Steven Kaplan noted in his book on French baking, *Good Bread is Back*, bakers in France were working towards a carefully conceived goal of excellent bread with a disciplined methodology as early as the seventeenth century. Bread culture developed through an inventory of structured recipes that demanded conscious control of the dough, with the goal of precise tastes and textures. At the time, elsewhere in the world, most people were still baking to fill empty stomachs, to survive. In his landmark cookery book, *Les Délices de la Campagne* (1654), Nicolas de Bonnefons, a valet at the court of Louis XIV, wrote: 'People of all nations . . . are in accord; in Paris one eats the best bread in all the world.' He was probably right: certainly, Parisians have been preoccupied with bread over all other food staples for centuries. Even today, French people are uneasy about the idea of a meal without bread.

The decline of French bread began during the Second World War. Following the armistice, and under pressure to keep prices down and the size of loaves up, French bakers started to take short cuts. In particular, they adulterated bread flour with added gluten, ascorbic acid and fava bean flour, to create dough that rose quickly and could withstand intensive, mechanized kneading, which forced oxygen in and bleached the natural carotenoids in flour out. More salt was then added, to compensate for the lack of taste. In trying to feed a broken nation, French bakers abandoned craftsmanship. Many other countries, notably Italy, suffered a similar implosion of baking standards at the same time. And, as the American chef Julia Child is ascribed with asking in a 1966 interview, 'How can a nation be called great if its bread tastes like Kleenex?'

Across the Channel from France, in 1961, a cabal of chemists, bakers and engineers from the Flour Milling and Baking Research Association, based in the leafy village of Chorleywood, near London, devised a new method of baking bread. They had been specifically tasked with creating a process that allowed small bakeries to compete with their industrial rivals, by making bread with British wheat (rather than Canadian imports), at low cost. The resulting system was called the 'Chorleywood Bread Process' (CBP). White flour made from relatively low-protein wheat, plus an assortment of additives, was subjected to high-speed mixing and baking, to produce a loaf that was softer, whiter, springier and cheaper than anything the British public had seen before. The entire operation, from raw flour to wrapped sandwich loaf, took three and a half hours – a fraction of the baking time hitherto. The new-style loaves had a longer shelf life too.

For fans, CBP bread was a marvel of Space Age food chemistry, a quotidian, edible touchstone of Harold Wilson's 'white heat of technology' era. Consumers loved it. They did not care that the bread was superficially attractive and artificially fresh, with the texture of candyfloss and the flavour of cotton. Very quickly, the majority of bread sold in the UK was made according to the Chorleywood Bread Process. Unfortunately, industrial bakeries were quick to adopt the novel, cost-saving method, ensuring the demise of the small bakeries it had been designed to save. In time, the process was exported. Today, CBP technology is used in over thirty countries from Ecuador to Australia and South Africa to Turkey. Over 80 per cent of the bread consumed in Britain is made this way.

For detractors, the CBP system is a crime against bread – a victory for expediency and profit over nutritional value and flavour. It is also, arguably, the endgame in the slow degradation of this human staple that began almost a century earlier, with the advent of roller milling. CBP bread has no taste, or at least it satisfies the lowest common denominator in taste, while it lacks structure or body. When a mollusc of gummy paste clamps to the roof of your mouth like a limpet to a rock in a stormy sea, you know you are eating CBP bread. As Elizabeth David wrote: 'A technological triumph factory bread may be. Taste it has none. Should it be called bread?'

The greatest disquiet today, however, surrounds the cocktail of chemicals that are routinely added to the usual quartet of ingredients – flour, water, salt and yeast – during the bread-making process. The baker and author Andrew Whitley has peered behind the opaque labelling on packets of industrial bread, documenting the long list of additives known within the industry – and without irony – as 'improvers'. These additives include hard fats, soya flour, acetic acid, powdered gluten, reducing agent (L-cysteine hydrochloride), flour-treatment agent (ascorbic acid), emulsifiers (mono- and diglycerides of fatty acids, sodium stearoyl-2-lactylate, glycerol monostearate, lecithins and others), bleaching agents, preservatives (calcium propionate) and enzymes. These additives – or adulterants, depending on your point of view – perform a variety of functions that encompass whitening the loaves, tightening gluten and retaining gas to increase volume, improving crumb softness, creating stretchier dough, inhibiting the growth of mould, reducing staling rates, emboldening crust colour and enhancing flavour. Between them, the additives substantially modify the cascade of chemical and biological reactions that take place when naturally fermented dough rises.

Whitley and other real-bread campaigners in Britain are particularly concerned about the use of enzymes in industrial baking. These introduced enzymes – amylase, protease, lipase, oxidase, transglutaminase and others – tend to have similar properties to the enzymes occurring naturally in wheat. Because enzymes are destroyed by the heat of the oven during baking, their use in bread was officially deregulated in 1996. Today, introduced enzymes are classified as 'processing aids'. Unlike with additives, though, there is no requirement to list them in the ingredients panel on the wrappers of industrially produced bread. Generally, these enzymes make hastily fermented dough hold more gas and lead to bread that stays softer for longer. But do they also have unintended, negative consequences? There is evidence to suggest that bakery enzymes may further reduce the nutritional value of wheat, and even alter wheat proteins altogether, making it toxic to people with gluten intolerance.

For bakers, the 'viscoelastic' properties of gluten are fundamental: when mixed with water, they help dough trap gases during fermentation, giving bread shape and texture. Gluten has been a part of the human diet for thousands of years. Throughout this period, however, a small percentage of the human population has suffered from a negative reaction to gluten, the most extreme form of which is coeliac disease.

Around one per cent of people in the industrialized world suffer from this intractable and protracted autoimmune disorder. Symptoms vary, but generally gluten triggers an immune response in genetically susceptible people that causes damage to the small intestine, leading to dangerously poor absorption of vitamins and nutrients from food. Coeliac can be life-threatening. Though the disease was first observed and named by the Greek physician Aretaeus of Cappadocia, who probably lived in the second century BC, it was only defined in detail near the end of the nineteenth century, while its relationship to gluten in bread was not established until the late 1940s. In the last fifty years, there has been a fourfold increase in the incidence of coeliac disease in the USA, a jump that cannot be explained entirely by improved awareness and screening. There is no cure. The only treatment for coeliac disease is avoiding gluten completely.

Recently, other forms of self-diagnosed susceptibility to gluten, known collectively as 'non-coeliac gluten sensitivity', have become much more widespread. It is difficult to understand why this is happening, when there are no specific diagnostic tests and little medical evidence to substantiate the increase. There are certainly people whose sensitivity to gluten leads to unpleasant symptoms, but this does not explain the extent of the 'gluten-free' trend. Over ten per cent of UK households are now gluten-free, while the value of gluten-free food sales in the USA alone in 2020 amounted to $23 billion. Switching to a gluten-free diet can trigger weight loss, which may explain the allure for some. No doubt others have been influenced by the rich and famous who go gluten-free: Miley Cyrus, Gwyneth

Paltrow, Bill Clinton, Rachel Weisz and Kourtney Kardashian have all dabbled in this form of food neuroticism. In the last decade or so, dietary fads like 'Paleo', 'wheat-belly', 'gluten-free' and others that use pseudo-science to make alarmist claims linking gluten to an array of illnesses including autism, depression, diabetes and Alzheimer's, have turned gluten into the *bête noire* of the wellness industry. In the process, bread has become demonized in a quasi-religious fashion.

The problem with many gluten-free diets, as medical researchers and doctors often now warn, is that they lack essential nutrients. Wheat has the highest protein content of any staple food apart from soy. Wheat is also an important source of micronutrients including B vitamins and selenium, minerals like iron and zinc, and dietary fibre (in wholemeal bread). The body of peer-reviewed scientific evidence on the relationship between bread and human health makes it clear that wholemeal bread has a beneficial effect.

It is, however, difficult to avoid the conclusion that the bread people ate in the pre-modern era was less challenging to their immune systems. Perhaps the Chorleywood Bread Process itself is actually making people unwell. A decade ago, I concluded that CBP bread – made with 'no-time dough', a cocktail of chemical adulterants including powdered gluten, large quantities of yeast and unspecified enzymes, and prepared with no regard for nutritional value or flavour – was making me unwell. I have not eaten it since, but I can eat sourdough bread that has been fermented slowly. The thinking here is that lactic acid bacteria break down gluten in a way that makes it easier to digest. Of course, the symptoms experienced by some people with non-coeliac gluten sensitivity might not be caused by gluten at all. There is a growing body of evidence indicating that the villain in certain gastrointestinal feuds might be a group of carbohydrates that are poorly absorbed in the small intestine, called FODMAPs.

There is also information suggesting that modern varieties of wheat, bred specifically for industrial bakeries, have more immunogenic compounds than heritage varieties, leading to a higher incidence of coeliac disease and other forms of gluten sensitivity in the twenty-first century. Nobody knows why. Perhaps our hybridizing practices since the 'Green Revolution', the seismic change in crop-breeding techniques and farming practices that boosted agricultural production in the developing world during the second half of the twentieth century, have been so persistent that we have created a plant that is now out of sync with developments in the human immune system and gut. As the late author and environmental activist Peter Matthiessen wrote in a different context: 'We have outsmarted ourselves, like greedy monkeys, and now we are full of dread.'

The father of the Green Revolution, Norman Borlaug, was born in Cresco, Iowa, in 1914. He came of age during the Dust Bowl, the period of drought and severe storms that wreaked havoc on the American and Canadian plains in the 1930s, precipitating an environmental and human disaster that led many to question modern agriculture. Not Borlaug. By 1944, the young agronomist was developing chemicals for a company called DuPont when he received an invitation from the

Rockefeller Foundation to work on an innovative project to improve crop yields in Mexico.

Thirty-five years prior to this, German chemists had first synthesized nitrogen and hydrogen to produce liquid ammonia. What became known as the 'Haber-Bosch Process' is arguably the most significant chemical innovation of the twentieth century. It led, in 1927, to the production of a breakthrough composite soil fertilizer, 'Nitrophoska' – a highly concentrated chemical form of nitrogen that farmers could feed to their soil. Nitrogen is a building block of all plant and animal tissue. It is the nutrient responsible for vegetative growth, and for the protein component in cereal grains, including gluten. Wheat pre-eminently demands nitrogen. Thus, for millennia, the availability of mankind's staple foods – significantly, bread – was naturally limited by the amount of nitrogen in the soil. Even though farmers did not know what nitrogen was until the late eighteenth century, they understood that their practices – growing leguminous plants like peas, lentils and clover (that fix nitrogen from the air) alongside wheat and barley; leaving land fallow; rotating crops; and, significantly, spreading manure (that contains nitrogen) on fields – all improved soil fertility. The problem was that, by the early twentieth century, with a growing global population and increasing pressure on agricultural production, organic fertilizers were simply running out. Nitrophoska solved this problem.

Fixing atmospheric nitrogen in the laboratory was chemistry's contribution to the maintenance of civilizations based on bread. When synthesized ammonia was applied to 'modern wheats' – new, high-yielding varieties specifically bred to perform well with chemical fertilizers – they thrived. Remarkable as it would have seemed to anyone who had farmed the earth at any time in the previous eleven millennia, the natural limits of crop growing had, in a little over two decades from 1927, become irrelevant. Those long-established farmers' practices were effectively redundant, and the era of agricultural monocultures had begun. Humankind had taken control of the nitrogen cycle, paving the way for an unprecedented explosion in human population. It has been estimated that 40 per cent of the global population today are alive because of the Haber-Bosch Process.

For Norman Borlaug, though, working in Mexico during the 1950s, the powerful effect of fertilizers presented a novel problem. As the wheat stalks grew quicker and the seed heads were heavier following the application of chemicals, the new plants were increasingly likely to fall over, or 'lodge' as farmers say, making harvesting either difficult or impossible. The answer was simple – shorten the stalks. In 1952, Borlaug began breeding 'dwarf' varieties of wheat in Mexico. It was not an entirely original idea. Short-straw wheat had been grown, on a small scale, in Japan and Italy during the nineteenth century. Borlaug, though, was ambitious to make it work at large scale. With a small team of scientists, he first developed a range of semi-dwarf hybrids that matured under the fertilizer regimen, showed resistance to common diseases, ripened at the same time, yielded well and were easy to harvest. By 1963, semi-dwarf varieties made up 95 per cent of the wheat crop in Mexico. The country's harvest had increased sixfold since Borlaug arrived. Mexico was even exporting wheat. The

Green Revolution, as it became known, a period of rapid, momentous change in global agriculture, was taking off.

Borlaug then turned his attention to the Indian Subcontinent. There, the ballooning population, political instability, an agricultural system that had failed to modernize and a succession of poor harvests had brought India and Pakistan to the brink of mass famine. In 1967, one fifth of the US wheat harvest was exported to India as emergency food aid. Unsurprisingly, Malthusianism was back in fashion. The American biologist Paul Ehrlich's controversial book *The Population Bomb*, which predicted millions would starve to death across developing countries in coming decades, was published in 1968. It was a bestseller. Presumably Borlaug refused to read it. Certainly, he never dealt in pessimism. He continued to breed new varieties of wheat and rice with genes that provided complex disease resistance, ideal maturing dates and stronger, even shorter stems. Farmers in India and Pakistan abandoned traditional practices, planted the new seeds and applied the required fertilizer and pesticide courses. Within a few years, the results were almost as incredible as in Mexico. Between 1965 and 1970, wheat yields in India increased by almost 70 per cent. By 1974, India was self-sufficient in food. A decade after that, India – a country that had, in the mid-60s, braced itself for the starvation of millions – became a net exporter of wheat. In 1970, Borlaug was awarded the Nobel Peace Prize – there is no food and agriculture prize – for his role in the Green Revolution. The Norwegian institute noted: 'More than any other single person of this age, he has helped to provide bread for a hungry world.'

Between 1970 and 2000, the Green Revolution continued to transform agriculture. The world food supply even began to grow faster than the population. At the same time, agribusiness and the chemicals industry profited hugely, largely through patenting new seeds, fertilizers and herbicides. The 'Borlaug hypothesis' – that higher agricultural productivity reduced the pressure to expand the land area planted to food crops – proved to be true. Advances in farming also indirectly reduced infant mortality, raised the health status of millions of children and lowered global food prices. By the end of the twentieth century, the Green Revolution had almost completely removed the grim spectre of mass famine from our planet. Some economists have estimated that Borlaug saved a billion lives.

Sorting out ancient problems frequently begets new ones, though. As dwarf wheats do not shade out weeds, herbicides had to be employed to control all unwanted vegetation. As entire farms, regions and even countries began to grow monocultures of genetically homogeneous plants, the threat of disease and pest epidemics also had to be controlled – with routine, preventative spraying of fungicides and pesticides. As early as the 1960s, environmentalists began to flag the negative consequences of the Green Revolution. The profligate use of chemicals caused the greatest alarm, initially. In *Silent Spring*, published in 1962, author and ecologist Rachel Carson crystallized emerging concerns about the harmful side effects – particularly on biodiversity, but also on human health – of modern pesticides like DDT, along with other chemicals used in cereal production. In time, it became apparent that the excessive reliance on a small number of agri-chemicals led to the development of hundreds of resistant pests, pathogens and weeds. Fertilizers were also disastrous for soil health, while the growth in irrigation of farmland seriously depleted groundwater sources in many countries. Furthermore, dwarf varieties, the 'wonder wheats', still failed under extreme weather conditions. When Borlaug began a campaign to extend the Green Revolution to Africa in the 1980s, environmental groups persuaded organizations like the Ford Foundation and the World Bank not to promote the use of chemical fertilizers, stymying his efforts.

At the same time, social scientists noted that the Green Revolution destroyed traditional agricultural practices, favoured larger, mechanized farms and reduced rural employ-ment, particularly for women and landless labourers, forcing them to migrate to cities. It led to individual and, to some extent, national dependence on a handful of western agribusi-nesses and creditors. Also, modern wheats turned out to be incompatible with organic farming systems. And, perhaps inevitably, we got drunk on high yields in the developed world, which led to inefficient practices like feeding grain to livestock, on a massive scale.

The millions of peasant farmers who had been saving seeds and effectively breeding their own landrace wheat populations worldwide, for millennia, have been replaced by a few hundred seed companies. More than 70 per cent of the wheat grown in all developing countries today carries genes that Borlaug developed in Mexico. In this context, the Green Revolution can be seen as the intense culmination of 150 years of genetic selection in wheat. Scientists and agronomists are today worried that, in breeding highly productive varieties in large monocultures, one of our basic food staples could be vulnerable to new and unprecedented epidemics.

The UN Food and Agriculture Organization estimates that 75 per cent of all crop varieties were lost during the twentieth century – an immense genetic resource, the value of which we are still learning to appreciate. Seed banks like the Svalbard Global Seed Vault in Norway are strategic in protecting the genetic material we have left, but we have more collecting to do, to future-proof our food supply further. Ancient cultivated and, equally importantly, wild varieties of wheat may be crucial sources of genetic resistance to insects, pests and diseases in coming decades. One project gathering plant gene material is focused on the Fertile Crescent and, in particular, on Karacadağ. The mountain where wheat was first domesticated still proffers a multitude of wild varieties. It is remarkable that, although the evolution of wheat as a crop to make bread for humans occurred an epoch ago, the genetics of its wild ancestors may still provide keys to the further improvement and even the safeguarding of wheat in the future.

Given that a global population of ten billion is now inevitable, and in the face of the climate emergency, the further intensification of wheat production in some parts of the world is unavoidable. Chemical fertilizers will continue to provide the bulk of nitrogen in developing countries for decades. It is still a long shot, but there is a growing expectation that genetically engineered wheat plants that can fix their own nitrogen may emerge from plant technology laboratories by

2050. Meanwhile, there is considerable scope to switch more food production to less chemically intensive methods in developed countries, reversing the erosion of genetic diversity in plants at the same time.

One of the most exciting things about learning to bake real bread had been reading about and even encountering some of the people who are trying to reverse both the genetic homogenization of wheat and the dystopian pursuit of yield at the expense of everything else. These people are putting 'culture' back into cultivation, and flavour back into bread. For Dr Steve Jones, a renowned wheat breeder at the Bread Lab, affiliated to Washington State University, yield and flavour are not in inverse proportion. The Bread Lab has become the unofficial headquarters for anyone in the USA who is interested in bread at its elemental level: the wheat seed itself. Jones's research shows that older varieties of wheat contain higher traces of micronutrients like calcium, iron and zinc, which are not only important for the human diet, but also give bread flavour. He is marrying desirable traits, using classical breeding techniques and technology, to create new varieties that both yield well – good for the farmer – and taste great, satisfying the consumer. The Bread Lab is breaking down the rigmarole of recent decades that says high-quality, nutritionally valuable food is necessarily expensive to produce.

In the British Isles, people like Ed Dickin, Andrew Whitley, the baker Kimberley Bell, Steven Jacobs and others at the UK Grain Lab, as well as Andy Forbes and John Letts, alongside an emerging coterie of young farmers and bakers, are all pursuing the same aim. Others are building on the work of the late

Martin Wolfe, a pioneer of low-impact cereal production who created a wheat population called 'ORC Wakelyns Population' or 'YQ' ('Yield and Quality'), which is now being grown around the country, in minutely adapted local variations. My neighbour in the Black Mountains planted ten acres of Wakelyns Population as I was writing this book. Elsewhere in the world, there are yet more activist farmers, breeders and bakers applying history, practical experience and science to hybridize heritage and modern varieties, and to create new landrace populations that will not only yield well in low-nitrogen environments and provide resilience in our changing climate, but also grow in organic systems and, significantly, add flavour, texture, cultural resonance and even respect to bread, once more.

I checked the oven temperature again – 230°C (446°F) in the centre of the hearth. Perfect. I flipped the first banneton over. The dough was ringed with concentric circles of flour, tinged with grey and Rubenesque. I had been baking in my wood-fired oven for several weeks, in batches of six or more loaves, which had improved my bread again. Using a razorblade, I quickly scored the skin of the dough four times. Employing my new dexterity with the peel, I thrust the plump dough into the back of the brick dome.

Scoring the dough just before it goes into the oven releases some of the surface tension, which permits controlled expansion as the dough heats up. Get it right, and the result is a loaf that blooms symmetrically and elegantly in the assigned places. Forget to do it, and the loaf will burst apart randomly at the weakest point. The slashes also serve as a kind of baker's signature. Poilâne loaves are signed with their famous inscribed 'P'. When villages shared communal bread ovens, common practice in Europe from the Middle Ages until the early twentieth century, the marks also identified which loaves belonged to whom. In medieval England, commercial bakers were required to mark their loaves with a distinctive stamp, in order to make any that contravened the law on weights and adulteration easier for the authorities to trace. Earlier still, one of the carbonized loaves found at Herculaneum, a town near Pompeii and also buried under ash and pumice when Vesuvius erupted, was imprinted with a stamp bearing the words 'Made by Celer, slave of Quintus Granius Verus'.

When the last, scored loaf was in place, I fixed the door tightly into the brick arch. Dough is alive until you cook it. In the oven, it goes through multiple changes, emerging as something entirely new – bread. Even though ten million loaves of bread are baked in the UK every day – a tiny proportion of the billions baked worldwide – we still don't completely understand the sequence of irreversible physical and chemical reactions that take place. This transformation of dough in the heat of the oven remains, at least in part, a mystery to us, just as it was to the first bakers thousands of years ago. I had read about these changes. I had even sat in front of glass oven doors and watched loaves baking for hours at a time, to witness with my own eyes the metamorphosis from dough to bread.

Landing on the hearth, the dough gives a ripple of intent, like a hibernating creature awakening in spring, before beginning to swell. The first wave of heat, transmitted by conduction from the brick, envelops it, fuelling the last climactic heave of furious fermentation. Steam hastens the transfer of heat to the dough during these first minutes. The steam also, critically, keeps the crust soft, allowing the dough to expand further. Initially, it grows horizontally, but without conviction. Then, as the millions of minute cells trapped in the dough balloon under pressure when alcohol and water vaporize into gases, the dough unfolds upwards. It rises in slow motion, like a rubber dinghy being filled with air from a foot pump. At the peak of its jubilant distension, the dough bulges and tears at the shoulders, where the baker has scored it with a razorblade. This final period of intense fermentation, known as the 'oven spring', will define the shape and texture of the loaf. It is a wondrous, exuberant last gasp of life before the yeasts and other organisms in the dough make the ultimate sacrifice.

When the yeasts have died and the temperature of the dough reaches 60°C (140°F), the starches swell with water, transforming the expanded dough into a throbbing, viscous mass. Still, the heat of the oven steals deeper into the dough. At 70°C (158°F), the compound chains of gluten coagulate like egg whites, and the structural development is complete: the interior of the loaf has reached its definitive constitution. When the temperature reaches 100°C (212°F), the remaining water in the dough evaporates. The crust is then formed via a complex chemical process called the 'Maillard reaction', by which proteins are broken down to combine with molecules of sugar and other products of fermentation, creating dozens of new aromatic compounds. As the crust hardens, it changes colour, unevenly, in waves: yellow to oatmeal, chestnut, amber, russet and then dappled cocoa. In the final act of this epic transformation, at around 150°C (302°F), dry heat causes sugars on the surface to crisp and caramelize. The bread is baked. An inedible, spiritless mixture of flour, yeast, salt and water blended into a pasty, greyish dough has been converted into life-giving sustenance – a golden, mouth-watering loaf of bread.

I extracted the first loaf with the peel and slipped it on to the worktop. Immediately, I began to apprehend the qualities of the bread with all five senses. Perhaps more than anything else, it is the smell of bread that has the most profound effect on us. It is one of the most recognizable food aromas on earth, and it never fails to lift my mood. The fragrance of sourdough bread is a complex amalgam of dozens of volatile chemical compounds generated primarily during fermentation, and then activated through baking. Prominent among the compounds are 2-acetyl-1-pyrroline, 2 N-heterocyclics, 6-acetyl tetrahydropyridine, maltol and isomaltol. It is hard to marry such prosaic names with a bouquet of smells that have stirred the emotions of humankind so keenly over millennia, but that is chemistry for you.

I inhaled deeply. I thought of Levin, who, in *Anna Karenina*, 'laughed and wept from joy' when 'the smell of baked bread wafted from the window'. The roasted odour – the smell most readily associated with bakeries, and which supermarkets artificially pump out, to put a spell on ingenuous shoppers – reached my olfactory nerves first. I inhaled again – there was caramel, malted buttery popcorn, spices, hazelnuts and honey. For the American food writer M. F. K. Fisher, the smell of bread was 'one of the world's sweetest smells . . . there is no chiropractic treatment, no yoga exercise, no hour of meditation in a music-throbbing chapel that will leave you emptier of bad thoughts.'

When all six loaves were on the cooling rack, I studied their colour, shape and texture. They were as good as anything I had ever baked. It was hard to choose between them, but I picked one out. I was finally ready for the Llanthony & Valley District Show.

'You won't win. It needs to be a white loaf. This is not San Francisco or even Shoreditch, you know. It's the Llanthony Valley. Coming down here with your fancy grains. No chance,' Ian, my neighbour, said when I bumped into him outside the main marquee. Ian is a home baker too. We have compared notes about baking before. He had clearly just entered his own loaf into the competition, and he did not welcome the threat posed by mine.

Inside the produce tent, there were rows of tables stacked with onions, broad beans, coloured potatoes, shallots, courgettes, giant marrows, rhubarb ('three sticks, trimmed'), 'funniest shaped vegetables', runner beans, dahlias, pansies, sweet peas, 'gent's buttonholes' and 'a single scented rose'. In one corner there were shelves of jars and bottles containing bucolic pick-me-ups and hedgerow elixirs like elderflower cordial, blackberry jam, haw jelly, quince jelly, sloe gin, rhubarb gin and damson vodka, all in a palette of colours that the Pre-Raphaelites might have painted with. There were tables with decorated wellies, 'vegetable monsters' and edible necklaces. In the centre of the tent, yet more tables groaned under the collective weight of sixteen classes of baking produce: decorated cupcakes, Welsh cakes, boiled fruitcakes, cheese scones, novelty cakes ('any size or shape') and carrot cakes ('men only'). The greatest number of entries were in the Victoria Sandwich class ('three-egg recipe; raspberry-jam filling only; cake can be sprinkled with caster sugar'). Finally, I found the table for 'Class 61: 2lb loaf of bread: white or brown'. There were five entries. Only one of them – a perfectly risen, crusty white cob – was a genuine contender. It was Ian's.

'Excuse me!' A stentorian female voice assailed me from the far end of the marquee. 'The public are absolutely not allowed to be in here. Judges only before 13.00 hours.' Advancing towards the lady, holding my loaf aloft like an Olympic torch bearer, I explained. Twiddling her glasses, she eyed me warily. I wondered for a moment if she thought I had been tampering with the other entries. Once she had placed a neat line through my name on her clipboard and pocketed my 50p entry fee, she ushered me out of the tent and into the brilliant sunshine.

Armed with a pint of cider, I ambled past the sheep-shearing demonstrations and the dog show area, round to the grass viewing bank above the main ring. Shortly after midday, the gun for the fell race sounded: two dozen sinewy men and women loped off up Hatterrall Hill. After the formal opening by the Show President, the 'Sports and Races' began: the mums' race, the dads' race, the sack race, the three-legged race and the 'four in a large sack' race passed off with great exuberance, hilarity and several pulled muscles. The three dog races ('under 15 inches'; '15 inches and over'; and 'open') raised the bar. A modest number of dogs did run in a straight line across the main ring, into the open arms of their bellowing owners. The greater number, however, seizing the day, headed directly for the picnic area or the burger van. When the canine chaos had finally abated, the gymkhana could begin.

By the middle of the afternoon, three pints of cider down, I had almost forgotten about my loaf and the competition. As the runners in the mile race lapped the main ring, I saw that the sides of the produce tent in the far corner of the field had been rolled up, and the public were swarming through. The judging was complete. I wondered if I should walk over and find out the result of Class 61. The Show was far from over. The parade of floats and the fabled rodeo were still to come. The bar would be open into the evening. I did not want disappointment to cloud the rest of the day. I was still mulling this over when I spotted Ian, pacing up the grass bank through the recumbent picnickers towards me.

'There will be an appeal of the judges' decision,' he was shouting, waving a sky-blue card in the air. 'You're basically a professional.' The blue card meant Ian had collected second prize. I whispered a prayer of thanks to the Roman bread-goddess, Ceres. I had won.

EPILOGUE:

Breaking Bread

'Bread is the only food that satisfies completely, all
by itself. It comforts the body, charms the senses,
gratifies the soul and excites the mind. A little
butter also helps.' – Jeffrey Steingarten

The sun was coming up over the hill, painting the fields on
the far side of the valley in a honeyed, auburn glaze. After
several days of thunderstorms and showers, the skies above
Wales had cleared and the dawn chill carried the first hint of
autumn. The weather forecast was excellent and, for many,
the wheat harvest would begin this week. Almost exactly a
year ago, I had been sharpening a sickle, in readiness for my
own harvest. A year before that, growing wheat to make bread
for my family had been no more than the kernel of an idea.
A pigeon clattered out of the lime tree above my head. With
two hands, I snapped the bread oven door open. A breath of
warm, scented air escaped through the brick arch. I thrust the
long-handled peel inside the dark dome and started to retrieve
my loaves.

It is difficult to fully understand the sense of triumph a fresh
loaf confers on the baker, but I know this: when my bread comes
out of the oven, the world is breaking someone else's heart.

Modifying grass into something edible and wholesome certainly satisfies a primordial urge. There is, moreover, attainment in making an article that did not exist before, and in creating order out of disorder. 'A loaf of bread is . . . an edged object wrested from the flux of nature – and specifically from the living, shining, Dionysian swamp that is dough. Bread is the Apollonian food,' Michael Pollan wrote. That a loaf of bread is also fragrant, risen and aesthetically pleasing is significant too.

While the loaves cooled, I began to tidy up around the oven. Historically, bread was never eaten warm. Up to the modern era, baking books and health manuals recommended that bread be eaten a day after baking, no matter how irresistible the smell. Science supports this. Bread continues to go through chemical changes while cooling. A loaf loses roughly 2 per cent of its weight, and the crust flakes slightly, while bread that cools slowly also stays fresh longer. Harold McGee noted in his seminal book, *On Food and Cooking*, that it takes a day for bread to reach its optimum condition for slicing. Lionel Poilâne insisted that his sourdough *miche* breads reached their peak three days after baking. I had no intention of waiting that long, though. I had risen early, to bake bread for a family lunch.

The six loaves piled up on the cooling rack were far from flawless. Some had lost their shape, with uneven growths around the edges where the heat had caused the dough to bubble; others had ripped open across the top, ignoring the marks I had scored with a blade. I reminded myself of Voltaire's aphorism: 'The perfect is the enemy of the good.' All the loaves were made with flour from the wheat I had grown, but I was near the end of it. I still had a sack of emmer grain that I milled in a countertop mill each time I baked, but the flour from Felin Ganol had run out, and I had no more Hen Gymro. My flour would just about last a year. I had baked over one hundred loaves with it and more than provided enough bread for the family; plenty of loaves had gone to friends too. When you tot it up, it is amazing what you get back from planting an acre of grain on a damp hillside in Wales. Occasionally, I had mixed the two types of flour together; at other times, I had added strong white organic flour from British millers, in my search for the best loaf. My two types of flour had incrementally distinct, technical baking properties. They also tasted differently. Before the modern era of hybridized wheat, dried yeast, steel roller mills and homogeneous flour, all bread would have tasted differently. We have largely forgotten this.

Heterogeneity is quietly returning to bread again. When my own flour did finally run out, I would certainly carry on baking with organic, stoneground, British-grown cereals with diverse qualities and flavour. Even five years ago, this would have been difficult, but today the choice is excellent, and expanding. In the future, I could be baking loaves of einkorn, rye, wholemeal spelt, Wakelyns YQ, Miller's Choice, Golden Drop, Red Lammas, Kent Old Hoary and Orange Devon Blue Rough Chaff, to name just a few of the varieties of flour available from small British millers. Real bread culture is stirring again. The number and the distribution of craft bakeries is rising across nearly all developed countries, while sales of industrially produced, sliced white bread continue to fall. At the same time, the number of home bakers is increasing too – a trend that accelerated exponentially during the coronavirus lockdown in 2020.

The understanding that a handful of wheat seeds plus water, sourdough starter and salt are all you need to produce an everyday, edible wonder is returning to the mainstream. However, in the UK, industrially produced, medium-sliced white bread remains a weapon in the supermarket wars, which means it is produced and sold very cheaply. And, despite the nutritional benefits of wholemeal bread, the majority of consumers still prefer the texture of white bread. History informs us that bread culture will shift again in the future, but real change in our dysfunctional food system is still some way off. To stem the river of deceit pouring from the industrial baking industry requires lawsuits, legislation and collective action from farmers, millers, bakers and consumers. But while we are waiting, we might as well eat great bread.

When the loaves had cooled, I sliced two of them in half at the kitchen table. Along with opening the oven door, this is the other 'big reveal' in the baking process: you see the 'crumb', or inside of the loaf, for the first time. Concepts of the ideal crumb manifest themselves in every aspect of bread making, from the variety of wheat and the freshness of the flour, to the leavening system and the recipe used. To expert bakers, the size, pattern, and even the pearly sheen of the holes, reveal information about how the dough was fermented and, more importantly, how the bread will taste: good architectural structure prefigures good flavour. Showboating bakers like my wife readily produce loaves with shiny, wild, uneven-sized holes running amok across the crumb, which gives bread a delightfully chewy quality.

In both my loaves, the crumb was pale brown, evenly baked and slightly moist. The holes, or 'alveoli' as some bakers call them, created by pockets of gases trapped in the dough during fermentation, were modest in size but well distributed. I thought about photographing the crumb and decided against it, just in case my children caught me in the act. When my daughter Scarlett had picked up my phone recently, I'd heard her say to Kitty: 'Dad's lock screen is a loaf of his own bread. How sad is that?'

As I lifted one of the hunks to smell it, my wife swung round to inspect. A slight purse of her lips indicated approval. Dozens of volatile chemical compounds, mainly derived from the metabolism of yeasts during fermentation, contribute significantly to the rich and tangled aromas of the crumb, which are different to the smell of the crust. The odour was floral, yeasty, malty, alcoholic and buttery.

To entice my three 'screen-age' children out of their bedrooms to eat, I left the cut loaves on a bread board by the kitchen door, from where the smell could climb the stairs. If that didn't work, I would employ the failsafe technique – turn the Wi-Fi off. By the time my wife and I had heated the soup, put cheese on a plate and made a salad, they had all drifted down and were making a fuss of their granny, my mum. We were not sitting down to a lavish banquet; it was just a Saturday lunch, but Mum was returning to her home and the kids were off to festivals and summer gatherings. It was the last meal we would take together for a while.

My kids think I obsess about eating communally, with your kith. The act is an ancient, universal form of civil intercourse with deep biological roots, and I stand by the aphorism attributed to Plutarch: 'We do not sit at the table to eat, but to eat together.' Communal eating enforces group belonging, promotes camaraderie, services friendships, shapes our ethics, strengthens communities, integrates strangers and engenders trust – you have to put down your weapon (or at least in our house, your iPhone) before pulling up a chair. It is trite to say that children learn manners at the dinner table. More importantly, they learn about mutualism, the doctrine that mutual dependence is necessary for social well-being. They witness generosity and experience the power of sharing, humankind's principal defence against need over aeons.

The demands and conveniences of modern times – long working hours, fast food, sport on smartphones, the fragmentation of our diet – have killed communal meals. Yet, eating face to face is more important than ever, as a counterpoint to the insulated, individualized structure of life on social media. Food also plays a significant role in the emotional narrative of our lives, or at least it should. As the philosopher Julian Baggini wrote: 'We are not so much what we eat, but what we remember we have eaten.' And we remember better when we share – or, to use an expression that is as ancient as it is common, when we 'break bread' together.

Companions are the people we break bread with. The word is derived from the Old French *compaignon*, literally 'one who breaks bread with another', and based on the Latin *com* ('together with') and *panis* ('bread'). The word exists in many languages from Spanish (*compañero*), Portuguese (*companheiro*), Italian (*compagno*) and Catalan (*companya*) to Bosnian (*kompanyon*), Georgian (*komp'anioni*), Finnish (*kumppani*), Russian (*kompan'on*) and Esperanto (*kompano*). Bread connects us, materially and symbolically. It connects us to nature, and to each other. Cut a loaf into slices and one becomes many; share those slices around a table and many come together, as one.

'Dad, too much,' my son said, as I expounded on the philosophical paradox of the part and the whole, waving a bread knife over the table. 'No one is interested. Can you please just cut the bread?' I allowed myself a moment of satisfaction: we eat first with our eyes, and he was starving.

The taste and flavour of real bread are determined by many variable elements: the oven temperature, fermentation times, the starter, the recipe, the wheat variety, the style of kneading, the age of the flour since milling, the coarseness of the millstones and the refinement of flour are all important factors. Of course, the baker who conducts these instruments in an intricate symphony of transformation plays his part too. Some believe that harvesting at precisely the right moment, when the moisture content is ideal, also bears upon flavour. There is even talk of 'terroir' among sourdough aficionados today. An expression from winemaking, terroir is the site-specific combination of soil, sunlight and climate that makes one vineyard different from its neighbour. It is difficult to talk about terroir in bread without sounding like a fanatic, but the link between soil health and flavour is substantiated by science: microscopic nutrients in soil combine to form complex phytonutrients like amino acids, esters and flavonoids in wheat, which provide the foundations of flavour. As heritage wheat plants have larger root systems and more leaf surface than modern varieties, they generate phytonutrients more efficiently.

I cut two hunks – one of each, Hen Gymro and emmer – into farmhouse slices and, with a quick blessing under my breath, passed the bread board round. I watched my mum cradle a slice on to her plate with both hands. We pick up bread with our fingers rather than a fork, and tactile sensitivity is an important, early assessment of quality. Across the table, my son, with a complete lack of sacramental regard, was already halfway through his first thickly buttered wedge.

As everybody's olfactory systems are different, flavour and taste in foodstuffs are highly subjective, while a pleasure repeated and committed to memory can play a more significant part in taste than the immediate experience itself. To complicate things further, the olfactory and gustatory properties of bread are elaborate, poorly understood at a theoretical level, and notoriously hard to describe, at least compared to many of the other things we familiarly consume.

I bit into a slice. I like to try bread without butter initially, to accentuate the primal act of tasting. The crust crackled between my old molars. The texture of the crumb was light enough, but it had heft too. Taste and flavour are distinct. Taste is restricted to the five qualities detected by the tongue – sweetness, saltiness, sourness, bitterness and savouriness (or 'umami'). Flavour is detected mainly through the sense of smell, in the olfactory bulb. Taste, then, gives you a sketch of the foodstuff you are eating; flavour, the more elusive element, fills in the seemingly limitless details and colour.

There was sweetness first, to get the enzymes in my saliva working, and saltiness; then the aromatic, acidic tang, the instantly recognizable taste of sourdough. As I chewed, the medley of delicate aromas created during the lengthy fermentation process began to flow, and olfactory dispatches were sent from the back of my mouth to the cerebral cortex in my brain. A rich, roasted nuttiness filled my sinuses first, then dried pears, butterscotch and toasted wheat. I let my mind roam with the flavours. I smelt a field at the end of a long, hot summer's day. I smelt harvest.

It was not exactly a Proustian moment. The industrial white bread I grew up on is largely devoid of the olfactory tags that inspire culinary childhood remembrances. However, eating the second, buttered slice of my bread did stimulate a surge of involuntary memories. I thought of Tarık, scuffing his loafers on the summit of Karacadağ. I recalled the cloudburst that drenched Roger and his horses, Betsy and Alf, ploughing my acre. I thought of my wavering belief as I scattered seed into the heavy, brown soil, and my boyish delight when rows of green leaves first emerged. I felt the gnawing, medieval ache in my back, stooping to cut wheat alongside Mohammed, in the Nile Delta. I watched the chaff catch in the wind and swoop in oblique shapes over the hedge. I heard the patter of wheat berries landing in the winnowing basket, the booming of the mill at Felin Ganol, and the sucking sound of wet dough slurping through Nicolas Supiot's paws.

As my reverie deepened, I thought of the many people who had shared their knowledge, and others who had bent their backs to my endeavour. My loaves were artefacts arising from

Simple Wholemeal Sourdough

Ingredients
600g organic wholemeal, stoneground heritage grain flour (or
500g wholemeal flour and 100g strong white organic bread
flour, if you want the loaves to rise more)
400g warm water
200g sourdough starter
6g flaked sea salt

Mixing and Kneading
Place the flour in a mixing bowl, make a well in the centre
and pour in the water. Mix thoroughly, until all of the ingredients have been incorporated. Leave for at least an hour.

Add the sourdough starter and salt to the bowl. Mix well.
Scrape the dough on to a work surface and, for several minutes, stretch and fold, lifting the corners of the dough into
the middle and pressing down lightly. The gluten network in
dough made with wholemeal flour is fragile: be gentle. Return
the dough to the bowl. After half an hour, repeat the stretching and folding. If you have time, repeat again.

Fermentation
Return the dough to the lightly oiled mixing bowl and cover
with a wet tea towel. Leave to ferment in a cool place for 8–12
hours. You will have to play around with the time, the

temperature in your own kitchen and the amount of sourdough starter to get the fermentation spot on.

Proving

Turn the dough out on a heavily-floured work surface. Carefully 'knock back' the dough by stretching and folding. Turn the dough over and shape it into a round *boule*, building tension into the skin with the edges of your hands. Flour the *boule* and turn it over into a well-floured proving basket or *banneton*. Leave to prove for 1–2 hours.

Baking

Heat the oven to 230°C. Place a cast iron bread pan or *cloche* in the oven. When it is hot, turn the dough out of the *banneton*, into the bread pan. Score or cut the surface quickly. Return the bread pan to the oven with the lid on. After 15 minutes, turn the oven down to 210°C. Bake for 35 minutes; remove the lid and bake for another 15 minutes.

Remove the pan from the oven, turn the loaf out on a wire rack and leave to cool for a few hours. Slice. Butter. Share. Enjoy.

Selected Reading

Though there are innumerable books on baking, finding good writing on the history of bread was harder than I imagined. *Six Thousand Years of Bread* by H.E. Jacob was first published in 1944, but the overarching sweep of the narrative and the scholarship make it an excellent place to start, even today, if you want to learn about the social context of bread over millennia. *Bread* by Scott Cutler Shershow is a gem, illuminating the cultural significance of bread in a series of essays. In *Good Bread is Back*, historian Steven Kaplan relates, often in meticulous detail, the fall and rise of prowess in French baking. I also enjoyed *Bread: A Slice of History* by John Marchant, Bryan Reuben and Joan Alcock. *White Bread: A Social History of the Store-Bought Loaf* by Aaron Bobrow-Strain is a fascinating insight into modern bread politics, and how America ended up with bread that is not bread. *On Food and Cooking: The Science and Lore of the Kitchen* by Harold McGee, *History of Food* by Maguelonne Toussaint-Samat, *The Art of Fermentation* by Sandor Ellix Katz, *Archaeology of Food: An Encyclopedia* and *The Oxford Companion to Food* by Alan Davidson are all scholarly reference works that I dipped into regularly.

Wheat in Great Britain by John Percival is an excellent introduction to the history of wheat-growing on these islands. In *Restoring Heritage* Grains, Eli Rogosa makes a passionate, if occasionally discursive case for bringing landrace wheat varieties back from the brink of extinction. On the subject of global food production, I reaped knowledge from *Feeding the Ten Billion: Plants and population growth* by L.T. Evans and *An Edible History of Humanity* by Tom Standage. The best book I have read on the epic history of milling is *Flour For Man's Bread* by John Storck and Walter Dorwin Teague. Noel Kingsbury's *Hybrid* is similarly monumental in scope, relating the history and science of plant breeding from the birth of agriculture to the present. In *The Third Plate*, chef Dan Barber shares his vision for a more enlightened way of eating, and what that might mean for agriculture and the soil. *Cooked: A Natural History of Transformation* by Michael Pollan is well researched and a pleasure to read.

I also enjoyed, for the writing as much as the recipes, *English Bread and Yeast Cookery* by Elizabeth David, *The Bread Baker's Apprentice: Mastering the Art of Extraordinary Bread* by Peter Reinhart, *Beard on Bread* by James Beard, *Bread Alone* by Daniel Leader and *Bread Matters* by Andrew Whitley.

Acknowledgements

The idea for this book germinated in the fertile minds of my wonderful agent, Rebecca Carter at Janklow & Nesbit UK, and my former editor at Particular Books, Helen Conford. Josephine Greywoode then took the reins to edit the first draft: she separated the wheat from the chaff, you might say, and guided the book assuredly to publication. My gratitude to the whole Penguin team, particularly in this instance Rebecca Lee, Liz Parsons and my indefatigable publicist, Annabel Huxley, is undiminished over ten years and three books.

I could never have undertaken a project of this scope without the advice and knowledge of a small legion of experts. I am, then, indebted to all the agronomists, farmers, millers and bakers who have either inspired me or generously shared their mastery and passion for growing wheat and baking bread. They include Jean Marc Albisetti, Sarah Andrews at Talgarth Mill, Syd Aston of Aston's Bakehouse, Paul and Ginny Baillie, Martin and Jill Cook at Cloddock Mill, Shane Donaldson, Rupert Dunn at Torth y Tir, Oscar Harding at Duchess Farms, Jonathon Harrington, Katie Hastings, Paul Hore of Harvest Support, Polly Hunter and Sophie Kumar at the Angel Bakery, Steven Jacobs at OF&G, Alan Jones, Simon Kitchen (for the flails), David Kuegler (for teaching me to scythe), Mark Lea at Green Acres Farm, John Lister and Chris Holister at Shipton Mill, Ben Mackinnon at e5 Bakehouse, Josiah Meldrun of Hodmedod's, Graham Morris, Professor Mark Nesbitt and Julia Adamson at the Economic Botany Collection, Royal Botanic Gardens, Mick Petts, Keith and Emily Powell, Nick Powell, Will Radmore, Slim, Roger Smith, Nicholas Supiot, Rachael Watson of the Abergavenny Baker, Andrew Whitley, Andrew and Sybille Wilkinson of Gilchesters Organics, the late Professor Martin Wolfe and Lexy Yorke (for Bernard).

I am particularly indebted to Dr Ed Dickin, for his patient explanations of plant breeding and selection; to Anne and Andrew Parry of Felin Ganol Watermill; and foremost, to Andy Forbes, for guidance on everything from sowing grain to baking times for bread. Ed, Anne and Andy all kindly found time to read the first draft.

In Jerusalem, I would have been lost without BZ Goldberg, Bentzine Roeber and Iris Saraf-Reinharts. Mustafa Gonen, Mahmut Yıldız and Tarık Yıldız were all invaluable during my travels in Turkey. Ahmed Hamed, Ahmed Ajami and Mohammed Abdul Rahman Maliji were superb hosts in Egypt. Jim Diebert and his team of custom harvesters could not have been more welcoming when I visited the Great Plains of the USA. James Suter, as well as Hazel, Freya and Arlo Evans all bent their backs at harvest time. Anthony Hanbury-Williams, Mike Higgins, Steve Hopkins, Tess Lewis and Rob Yorke spontaneously provided snippets of poetry, learned articles and literary bread references.

Finally, finally, I would like to thank my children, Lucas, Scarlett and Katrina for their hours in the field and forbearance in the face of some dodgy loaves. Once again, my greatest debt is to my wife, Vicks, who first taught me to bake. In the words of Omar Khayyám (translated by Edward Fitzgerald):

> A jug of Wine, a Loaf of Bread – and Thou
> Beside me singing in the Wilderness –
> O, Wilderness were Paradise enow!

ALLEN LANE
an imprint of
PENGUIN BOOKS

Also Published

Joseph Sassoon, *The Global Merchants: The Enterprise and Extravagance of the Sassoon Dynasty*

Clare Chambers, *Intact: A Defence of the Unmodified Body*

Nina Power, *What Do Men Want?: Masculinity and Its Discontents*

Ivan Jablonka, *A History of Masculinity: From Patriarchy to Gender Justice*

Thomas Halliday, *Otherlands: A World in the Making*

Sofi Thanhauser, *Worn: A People's History of Clothing*

Sebastian Mallaby, *The Power Law: Venture Capital and the Art of Disruption*

David J. Chalmers, *Reality+: Virtual Worlds and the Problems of Philosophy*

Jing Tsu, *Kingdom of Characters: A Tale of Language, Obsession and Genius in Modern China*

Lewis R. Gordon, *Fear of Black Consciousness*

Leonard Mlodinow, *Emotional: The New Thinking About Feelings*

Kevin Birmingham, *The Sinner and the Saint: Dostoevsky, a Crime and Its Punishment*

Roberto Calasso, *The Book of All Books*

Marit Kapla, *Osebol: Voices from a Swedish Village*

Malcolm Gaskill, *The Ruin of All Witches: Life and Death in the New World*

Mark Mazower, *The Greek Revolution: 1821 and the Making of Modern Europe*

Paul McCartney, *The Lyrics: 1956 to the Present*

Brendan Simms and Charlie Laderman, *Hitler's American Gamble: Pearl Harbor and the German March to Global War*